"Read this book and unleash the heart of your marriage! Greg and Shawn have made it easy. From the first few pages you'll see that their approach is warm, engaging, practical and biblical. You'll want to read this book with your whole heart."

—Drs. Les and Leslie Parrott, founders of RealRelationships.com and authors of *Love Talk*

"I wholeheartedly endorse *The Wholehearted Marriage*! Greg Smalley and Shawn Stoever get to the heart of great marriages in this creative and engaging book. Their personal stories reveal heart-to-heart communication. Couples will understand why our hearts become closed and how to reopen them. In the end, couples will know how to care for both their heart and their partner's heart."

—David H. Olson, PhD; CEO of Life Innovations and codeveloper of the *PREPARE/ENRICH* Program

"If you have a teachable heart, *The Wholehearted Marriage* will give you just what the doctors have ordered: a clear message of hope, a roadmap to a healthy marriage, and a passion for restoration. Read it. Pray over what you have learned. Live it. Pass it on. Your marriage and those that you care about will win by your investment."

—Dr. Gary and Barb Rosberg, America's Family Coaches, authors of *6 Secrets to a Lasting Love*, radio show cohosts, and speakers

"*The Wholehearted Marriage* gives great insight on how to be fully engaged in your life and your marriage. Smalley and Stoever show how to deal with the disillusion, disappointment and heartbreak of life, so that past hurts do n[...] your future relationships. They demonstrate [...] heart issues, and share life-giving [...] struggling marriage."

—Mark Gungor, pastor, motivational speaker, CEO of Laugh Your Way [...]

The Whole*hearted* MARRIAGE

Fully Engaging Your Most Important Relationship

Dr. Greg Smalley and Dr. Shawn Stoever

HOWARD BOOKS
A DIVISION OF SIMON & SCHUSTER
New York   London   Toronto   Sydney

Our purpose at Howard Books is to:
* *Increase faith* in the hearts of growing Christians
* *Inspire holiness* in the lives of believers
* *Instill hope* in the hearts of struggling people everywhere
Because He's coming again!

Published by Howard Books, a division of Simon & Schuster, Inc.
1230 Avenue of the Americas, New York, NY 10020
www.howardpublishing.com

The Wholehearted Marriage © 2009 by Greg Smalley

In Association with Lee Hough and the Literary Agency of Alive Communications

Library of Congress Cataloging-in-Publication Data

Smalley, Greg.
The wholehearted marriage : fully engaging your most important relationship / Greg Smalley and Shawn Stoever.
p. cm.
1. Marriage—Religious aspects—Christianity. 2. Marriage. I. Stoever, Shawn. II. Title.
BV4596.M3S638 2009
248.8'44—dc22
2008054186

ISBN 978-1-4165-4482-1
ISBN 978-1-4391-6492-1 (ebook)

1 3 5 7 9 10 8 6 4 2

Manufactured in the United States of America

For information regarding special discounts for bulk purchases, please contact: Simon & Schuster Special Sales at 1-866-506-1949 or business@simonandschuster.com.

The Simon & Schuster Speakers Bureau can bring authors to your live event. For more information or to book an event, contact the Simon & Schuster Speakers Bureau at 866-248-3049 or visit our website at www.simonspeakers.com.

Edited by Jeff Gerke
Interior design by Davina Mock-Maniscalco

This book is dedicated to our wives,
Erin Smalley and Christina Stoever,
who laugh, play, love, live, and even sleep wholeheartedly.

Contents

Acknowledgments

FIRST AND foremost, we thank our Lord Jesus Christ, who fills our hearts with His amazing love.

This book could not have been completed without the help of many family, friends, and colleagues.

Thank you to our families, who have always cared about and supported our hearts and passions.

Thank you to the Smalley and Stoever children—Taylor Smalley, Taylor Stoever, Maddy Smalley, Cade Stoever, Garrison Smalley, and Cody Stoever—for the special gift of being your fathers.

Thank you to Jeff Gerke, an exceptionally gifted writer, for being our editor.

Thank you to Lee Hough of Alive Communications for his outstanding help in bringing this project to reality.

Thank you to Greg's colleagues at the Center for Relationship Enrichment—Gary Oliver, Jan Phillips, Jackson Dunn, Sherri Swilley, Judy Shoop, and Stew Grant—for your support in the writing of this book.

Acknowledgments

Thanks to Shawn's friends and colleagues at WinShape. You truly are amazing at transforming lives through relationships.

Thank you to the counselors and staff at the National Institute of Marriage, Battlefield Ministries, and Center for Relational Care.

Thank you to Howard Books and Denny Boultinghouse for your partnership and bringing our passion for married couples to life.

And, finally, thank you to the Howard Books and Simon & Schuster teams who have engaged in copyediting, internal design and layout, cover design, and the myriad of details required to bring this book to press.

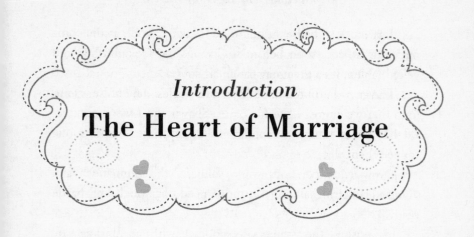

Introduction
The Heart of Marriage

ONE OF the most terrifying experiences of my professional life happened when Shawn and I (Greg) were speaking to a large group of Army Rangers and Special Forces soldiers (Green Berets) and their wives. If that wasn't intimidating enough, try keeping your composure when the commanding officer walks in and dead silence fills the room.

In all my life I've never witnessed as rowdy a crowd of grown men grow so quiet so quickly. You could literally hear a pin drop. Shawn and I gave each other one of those looks that says, "What in the world have we gotten ourselves into?"

Before I continue, let me give you a little background. Shawn and I are both psychologists with doctorates in clinical psychology. We have been counseling married couples in crisis and leading marriage-enrichment seminars for years. We've traveled the world helping couples learn how to have great marriages. And in that time we've seen and heard it all. At least that was what we thought until we agreed to do a marriage seminar at a U.S. Army Special Forces base.

That's not so bad, you might be thinking. Well, as the commanding officer stood before his troops, he looked at us and yelled, "Men, it's a great day for an air strike!"

The crowd erupted in cheers and whistles. The noise was so loud that we almost dove for cover. Shawn and I were stunned. I'd had some unique introductions in my time, but this one topped them all.

"Now remember, boys, you're soldiers," the commander said. "Don't go getting all soft on me. I need you tough and battle ready!"

In unison, the soldiers responded with an enthusiastic "Hooah!"

"Good job, men," he shouted back. "Now let me introduce your speakers . . ."

I must admit that I had no desire to leave the comfort of that old, rusty metal chair I was sitting on. But like a true gentleman, Shawn nudged me toward the podium. "Don't forget that they are trained to kill," Shawn whispered with a big smile. "And don't look them straight in the eye either. Don't worry, you'll be fine. Now go, go, go!" I felt like I was being pushed out of an airplane.

And with those words of encouragement, Shawn left me alone to face the hardened crowd of trained killers. Amazingly, even the wives looked tough. To make matters worse, my first talk was called "The *Heart* of Marriage."

We know what you're thinking. Why didn't we start with something easy like communication, conflict, finances, or sex? Surely "sex" would have been a real crowd pleaser!

The truth is that there was no place we could have started our seminar other than talking about the heart. It's like what Isaiah said: "The Spirit of the Sovereign LORD is on me, because the LORD has anointed me to preach good news to the poor. He has sent me *to bind up the brokenhearted*, to proclaim freedom for the captives and release from darkness for the prisoners" (Isaiah 61:1).

We think the world is like that commanding officer at the army base. The world wants us to live life without our hearts engaged, to ignore our hearts, and to believe that it's not manly to talk about our hearts. But the good news is that we don't have to live life *brokenhearted*. God desires that we fully engage our lives and marriages *wholeheartedly*.

LIFE WANTS TO BREAK OUR HEARTS

Kids are amazing. They laugh until their stomachs hurt, play until their bodies give out, cry until their eyes are red, and sleep like they haven't a care in the world. They fully engage every moment. They live life wholeheartedly.

I (Shawn) was driving down the road a few months ago when I overheard my eight-year-old son, Cade, yelling at his Game Boy. I attempted to use logic, telling Cade that the game could not understand what he was saying. He replied, "That doesn't stop you from yelling at the players on the television."

He had a point.

I asked what he was mad about. He explained that the defensive player on his handheld computer football game was upsetting him because he was not hustling. The computer player would not dive to make a tackle, and that made no sense whatsoever to Cade. In his world, you do everything full-out. If someone is getting past you in football, you dive. Wholeheartedly. No question about it.

We were all designed to live life like this. Full-out. With all of our hearts.

And we do . . . until the world gets a hold on us. The "world" may take on many forms—a parent's voice, unspoken expectations, traumatic events, pressure from peers—but the message is the same: Don't laugh so much; it draws attention. Don't play so long; you need to be serious. Don't cry so much; life is tough for everyone. Don't sleep so long; there is work to be done. Don't dive; it's not worth the effort. Be content, settle, compromise.

There are the occasional brave souls who continue to live with childlike wholeheartedness despite the world's efforts to undermine them. We call these people heroes.

Okay, maybe that's a little dramatic, but think about it. Who is your favorite athlete, performer, or artist of all time? As you picture that person in your mind, think about what you most admire about him or her.

We have asked audiences this question for years and have heard a multitude of responses. Heroes mentioned have been John Wayne, Lucille Ball, Tiger Woods, Carol Burnett, Frank Sinatra, John Wooden, Jimmy Stewart, Condoleezza Rice, Pistol Pete Maravich, Ronald Reagan, Bill Cosby, men and women serving in the armed forces, and many more. The reasons these people were admired were equally varied. Some respected the person's work ethic or service history or value system.

Only one thing seems to come across as universal: those individuals we deem our favorites *fully engage* with whatever they are called to do with their lives. Lucille Ball and Carol Burnett's fun-loving spirit, Tiger Woods and Pistol Pete's passion to practice, Condoleezza Rice and Ronald Reagan's wise leadership, Frank Sinatra and Jimmy Stewart's sincere performances, members of our armed forces and their spouses for their bravery and sacrifice . . . they all have lived wholeheartedly. We admire people who live life wholeheartedly—fully engaging, giving 100 percent, without reservations.

Growing up with my dad, I (Shawn) learned that people have the ability to put out effort in one of three ways:

♡ *Heartless effort.* When I was a kid, my dad would take me onto the construction sites he supervised in downtown Houston. I loved the enormity of the multistory buildings and the personalities of the people working to build them. My dad knew many of the employees by name and took it upon himself to know something each one cared about so that he could carry on a conversation with each worker as we passed. However, there were some we passed with a simple "hello." Dad explained that there were many people who worked just to collect a paycheck. They were good people, but their hearts were not in their work. Their effort was *heartless*.

♡ *Halfhearted effort.* I grew up playing Little League baseball. My sister was a cheerleader. My dad supported us both in our passions and rarely criticized—unless I only jogged when I hit a groundball that I knew would lead to an out even if I ran hard, or if my sister wanted to skip practice because she was not into it that day. Dad made it clear that we were not just to go through the motions, participating only *halfheartedly*.

♡ *Wholehearted effort.* Dad's hero was Nolan Ryan. Nolan was a Texas rancher, small-town boy, humble leader, and competitive baseball player. Nolan holds the record for the most strikeouts and the most no-hitters in Major League Baseball history. He pitched through fatigue and did whatever his coach asked him to do in order to help his team win. He did everything *wholeheartedly*.

The same three categories of effort are available to us. No matter what the topic—work, friendships, faith, hobbies, marriage—we get to choose what amount of heart we want to include in our effort.

I will frequently sit down to watch HGTV with my wife, Christina. My body is on the couch beside her, but my heart is definitely not into what we are watching. I recently played a flag-football game at our church. With a bad knee to start and a wet field, I definitely put out a halfhearted effort at making some of those tackles (and hoped my son was not watching to yell at me for not diving).

Yet when I watch my kids' activities, it is a different story. Then I am wholeheartedly cheering and encouraging as I watch Taylor at an acting performance or Cade in a baseball game.

How about you? Consider the following scale:

1	2	3	4	5	6	7	8	9	10
No Heart			Halfhearted				Wholehearted		

_____ Rate your effort *at work*.
  "Whatever you do, work at it with all your heart, as working for the Lord, not for men." (Colossians 3:23)
_____ Rate your effort *with God*.
  "Love the Lord your God with all your heart and with all your soul and with all your mind and with all your strength." (Mark 12:30)

_____ Rate your effort in *your marriage*.
"I [God] will give them an undivided heart and
put a new spirit in them; I will remove from them
their heart of stone and give them a heart of flesh."
(Ezekiel 11:19)

How did you do? If you are like most people, you scored
below a ten in each area. All of us admire people who live wholeheartedly and we aspire to live this way ourselves, yet we fall
short.

We're not wholehearted, we're *brokenhearted*.

WHOLEHEARTED MARRIAGE

In the Great Commandment God calls us to live wholeheartedly,
directing us to love Him and others *with all our heart*. We are
also told that the very reason Jesus came was so that we could
experience the fullness and abundance of life (see John 10:10).
Living wholeheartedly means fully engaging your heart in
whatever is before you. The benefits include maximizing the
effective use of your gifts and talents, experiencing true joy in
your life, and finding real fulfillment in your marriage.

Remember those old coaches of yours who used to yell, "Get
your head in the game"? God is up there on the big sideline, calling out something different: "Get your *heart* in the game." Fully
embrace your life.

The heart is the key to a fully engaged life and marriage.
We see this when we do marriage intensives with couples on the
brink of divorce. Couple after couple sitting across the room at-
tests to the fact that living a life without the heart engaged is
less than fulfilling. Money, fame, success, possessions, even rela-

tionships are meaningless if our hearts are not part of the process.

So you get it, right? The heart is important. Living wholeheartedly is vital, and you would like to do it. But what does all this have to do with marriage?

It has *everything* to do with marriage. A marriage without heart is not a marriage at all. Without heart, spouses are left in empty, disconnected, coexisting relationships. They complain to friends or come to counseling with a multitude of issues that all end up sounding similar: "We just don't connect anymore," "Our marriage has no passion," "My spouse does not really want me," "I feel alone in my own house," or "I'm not *in love* anymore."

All these statements are the result of a relationship without heart. These couples may go their separate ways or they may just stay in empty marriages to honor their covenant commitments. But either way, this situation isn't God's best for them.

Maybe this is why you picked up this book—you feel disconnected and alone in your marriage or your marriage is in crisis. Perhaps you have a good marriage but it has stagnated or you want to get back to a deeper level of intimacy and a higher level of passion—you want to take it from good to great. No matter where you are, the way to have the marriage you've always dreamed of *requires two hearts fully open and engaged.*

Even as I (Shawn) was working on this book, I paused to meet with a man from our church. Sam has an eighteen-year marriage and three boys. For years Sam believed he was being a good husband and father by providing financially for his wife and kids. He worked with a passionate intensity that often left him exhausted on the weekends. His wife watched him put his whole heart into his work, but she never felt that same level of engagement in their relationship. She longed for intimate connection with him.

Sam came by to tell me that his wife was filing for divorce. He now sees how she needed his heart in their marriage, but all she got was his resources and his mind. He is finally ready to engage his heart in their relationship, but she says it is too late. She is tired of being hurt and rejected. Her heart has hardened, and she no longer has the desire to continue. Sam and his wife are yet another tragic example of the state of many of our marriages: brokenhearted, halfhearted, or heartless relationships that end in pain and grief.

There is another option: you can learn how to reenergize your marriage by *fully engaging your heart*.

With hearts engaged, spouses are free to love without reservations. They become interested in fully pursuing each other, which communicates desire and makes the spouse feel wanted.

Passion *energizes* the marriage, allowing both spouses to connect deeply. Openness *characterizes* the marriage, so that true intimacy can occur. You hear statements like "I am so in love with my spouse," "I feel more connected than ever," "My home is the safest place on earth," and "My spouse is so passionate and romantic." In short, hearts fully engaged lead to *thriving* marriages.

Remember the words you used on your wedding day to pledge your heart to each other? Perhaps they sounded something like this:

I love you. You are my best friend.
Today I give myself to you in marriage.
I promise to encourage and inspire you, to laugh with you,
and to comfort you in times of sorrow and struggle.

I promise to love you in good times and in bad,
when life seems easy and when it seems hard,
when our love is simple, and when it is an effort.
I promise to cherish you and to always hold you in highest regard.
These things I give to you today, and all the days of our life.

These words cast the vision of a wholehearted life together. You and your spouse committed to this. More important, you and your spouse deserve this kind of marriage.

So what's the problem? God created us to fully engage life. We admire people who live wholeheartedly. Marriages reach their full potential when hearts are engaged. And yet, as the self-test above indicated, we are not living wholeheartedly. Why, if it is so important, are our hearts not engaged fully?

Through life experience and years of counseling, we have identified two key forces acting to prevent us from living wholeheartedly in our lives and marriages: (1) you have an Enemy out to destroy your heart, and (2) life circumstances work to isolate your heart.

One reason we sometimes don't fully engage life and marriage is that we have an Enemy who will not stop in his relentless effort to separate us from our hearts. In the same verse that Jesus tells us He came to give us life to the fullest, He also warns us that there is a thief (the Enemy) who comes to rob, kill, and destroy (see John 10:10). This Enemy robs us of abundant life by cutting us off from our hearts. He delights in seeing us disengage our hearts in our marriages so that we end up settling, compromising, surviving, or simply giving up.

The Bible tells us that the heart is the wellspring of life, the place we connect with God, the essence of who we are, and our connection point with others. If the heart is this important, it makes sense that the Enemy would level his greatest attacks there.

How does the Enemy do it? How does he take out something that is so important to us? He often uses the pace of modern life to rob us of meaningful, connected, wholehearted relationships. Psychiatrist Carl Jung once said, "Hurry is not of the devil, hurry is the devil." And he said that in the early 1900s. Our world now is faster than ever. Hurry is a way of life in our culture today. Think about it: How many times have you been in a hurry this week? Can you count them? Did you run out of fingers?

You were not designed to live life in a rush all the time. You were designed to slow down, enjoy, appreciate, and engage. We have in our DNA thousands of years of sitting and talking around a campfire, so why do we run around all the time like our pants are on fire?

That's what the Enemy wants—you frantically doing life at ever-increasing speeds with little understanding of the toll it is taking on you and your marriage. But you *can* slow it down and wholeheartedly embrace life. Or you can let him speed it up and rob you of real intimacy.

In addition to the hectic pace of life, the Enemy loves to attack by getting us to settle for less than God's best for our marriages.

In the bestselling business book *Good to Great* Jim Collins studied Fortune 500 companies to determine which ones made the leap from good to great.[1] After years of study, he chose to begin his book with the following sentence: "Good is the enemy of great." This is true in business, true in life, and true in marriage.

In marriage, to get from "near divorce," to "surviving,"

to actually having a good marriage takes a lot of investment and work. The easiest thing in the world to do then is become content with a merely "good" marriage and settle for where you are.

We are wired for more than "good." We were designed to pursue greatness in our marriages. But we look around and don't see many people up at "great." There are few role models. Not many people to hang out with in the Great Marriage category. So we settle.

Like most of Jesus' disciples on the lake, we decide to stay in the safety and comfort of the boat. Very rarely do we see someone stepping out in faith, like Peter walking on water, attempting to do something great. Wholehearted marriages take that courageous step toward greatness.

The first thing working against your marriage is the Enemy. The second thing consists of the traumas and life circumstances that come at us. These crises work to disconnect us from our hearts—the essence of who we are. I (Shawn) know about this stuff firsthand.

My mom and dad were both on the rodeo team in college. Yes, the rodeo team. They were full-time cowboys. My mom was actually one of the best cowgirls in the country, finishing second in the nation in the all-around competition at the National Finals. They both wholeheartedly pursued the activities they were passionate about. I grew up going to the farm with my parents on weekends, riding horses and working cattle. It was an amazing childhood.

My life as I knew it changed forever at age eight. My mom was having a persistent pain in her leg, so she reluctantly went to the doctor. My little sister and I sat in the waiting room for what seemed like an eternity as the doctors ran tests on my mom. When all the exams were completed, Mom herded us out into the car. We climbed into the backseat and waited for mom to start the car. She just sat there, staring ahead, before finally bursting into tears. It was the first time I had ever seen my mother cry. I didn't know what to do, what to say, or what to make of it. Later, we were told that mom found out she had bone cancer in her leg.

We lived in Houston, Texas—home of M. D. Anderson, the best cancer-treatment and research center in the world back in the 1970s. The doctors were great. Unfortunately, the psychologists were not. The prevailing theory on childhood grief at the time said that the best way for a child to remember a dying relative was in that person's healthiest state. Therefore, kids were not allowed in the hospital.

From the time of her diagnosis to her death, my mom lived nine months. In that period we got to see her only a handful of times. On November 1, 1978, I turned the corner onto our block, walking home from school, and spotted my parents' Suburban in our driveway. I sprinted the hundred yards to my door, excited to see my mom. As I walked in, I saw my dad was alone. We waited on my sister so he would have to share the news only once. Mom had died.

Eight-year-old boys think they are bulletproof. They believe they can put a sheet on, jump off the roof, and fly around for a while before landing gracefully. My wholehearted, fearless existence ended with the loss of my mom. The person who meant more to me than anyone else in the world had been in need, and I'd been helpless to offer a cure.

I now know that I responded to that tragedy the way countless others have done. I closed my heart down, walled it off, and made an unconscious decision to protect myself. Loving my mom wholeheartedly had led to more hurt and grief than I ever could have imagined. Something inside me said, "Don't you dare let that happen again."

That powerful negative life circumstance completely disconnected me from my heart. I was robbed of my connection to the wellspring of life, the essence of who I was.

Looking back, I can see how the next fifteen years of my life were powerfully affected by this. I quit playing team sports. I just did not want to be around anyone. About the only sport I played anymore was golf. I enjoyed golf because I didn't have to talk to anyone. Actually, golf is a pretty good game for someone disconnected from his heart. That way, feelings and emotions don't get in the way of analyzing your way around a course and executing shots. Look at most of the guys on the PGA tour: they look like robots.

Since my mind still worked, I was successful at golf and at school. But without a heart, my relationships were horrible. I treated people poorly, couldn't commit in dating relationships, had no self-esteem, and always felt lonely.

Midway through graduate school, I met a girl in a bar one night. She captivated me. She lived her life with reckless abandon. She was fun, exciting, and passionate. She also had a value system and an understanding of who she was that guided her decisions. I was drawn to her and the way she lived. In retrospect, I now understand that she fully engaged life.

We dated for a couple of years before she finally gave up on me. She was unwilling to continue in a relationship with a man who was all head and no heart. I was devastated. It forced me to finally come face-to-face with the biggest decision of my life: Would I continue protecting myself, keeping my heart out of any relationships. Or was I willing to risk being hurt, exposing my heart and truly connecting?

After a lot of prayer and wrestling with God, I chose the latter path. It took two more years to convince that girl that I was really going to do relationships and life with my heart engaged. I finally wore her down, and in a leap of faith on her part she married me. Fourteen years later, Christina still holds me accountable for engaging my heart in our marriage.

This short version of my story gives you a glimpse into how life circumstances can be used to disconnect us from our hearts. We each have a story.

I had a history teacher who liked to say, "Those who do not learn from the past are destined to repeat it." I was in high school, so I thought he meant we would have to retake the class if we didn't study. Turns out, he meant a lot more than that. Our pasts, our histories, our stories are what make us who we are. Learning from our pasts is not about blaming someone else for what has happened: "I'm messed up because of my parents." Studying our pasts is about understanding the role of our hearts in life, how they have been attacked, and what we have done to protect them.

Sometimes the traumatic events in our pasts are pretty evident. The child whose parents divorce. The little girl who is sexually molested. The little boy whose mom dies. Other times they may be more subtle. The kid who is picked on because he is different. The little girl who is not as pretty as the others. The little boy with no athletic ability. Regardless of the situation, none of us escapes childhood without some wounds.

These wounds lead us to protect ourselves. That protection takes the form of closing down our hearts and pushing people away. That closing down prevents us from fully engaging in life and relationships. That halfhearted effort in relationships leads to poor marriages and often divorce.

LOOKING FORWARD

Unfortunately, a disengaged, protected heart makes it impossible to experience an intimate, connected marriage. Closed hearts block the flow of love. Couples drift apart. We settle, compromise, and find some version of contentment. Or worse, we end up living in survival mode, defending ourselves in response to the difficulties of our circumstances. Or still worse, we give up and go looking for love somewhere else.

Living wholeheartedly is difficult to achieve but worth the effort. A short list of the benefits of fully engaging the heart includes these:

♡ you overcome your past life circumstances to wholeheartedly live the life God designed you for;

♡ you experience true intimacy and passionate connection with your spouse, leading to an amazing marriage;

♡ you fully engage in genuine fellowship and community with the family and friends around you;

♡ you serve the Lord and lead a revival in your church with authentic people attracting and ministering to the lost.

After reading *The Wholehearted Marriage*, you will know how to reconnect with your desire to live wholeheartedly and experience a fully engaged marriage.

Throughout this book, our goal is to help you understand the heart, value it, take care of it, and use it to bless your spouse. Specifically, we will help you:

1. understand your heart and its role in marriage;
2. unclog your heart so you can reengage it in life and in your marriage; and
3. unleash your heart to empower your spouse to live wholeheartedly.

Whatever the details of your story, you are reading this book because you want to have the best possible marriage. We commend you for your hope and desire, and so we say, "Have a wholehearted adventure!"

PART ONE

Understanding the Heart

Chapter 1
Heart 101

The "heart" refers to its position in the human being, as the center or core to which every other component of the self owes its proper functioning.
—Dallas Willard, *Renovation of the Heart*

Oh, that their hearts would be inclined to fear me and keep all my commands always, so that it might go well with them and their children forever!
—Deuteronomy 5:29

T RUST ME."

I (Greg) can't tell you how many times those two little words have come back to haunt me. Usually when people say "Trust me," what they really mean is "I have no idea what I'm talking about or what I'm getting us into, but this seems really fun, and I think we should do it anyway!"

Sadly, in this case the "it" referred to my marriage, and the "trust me" was spoken to convince my fiancée, Erin (my wife now

21

of seventeen years), that our most recent argument wasn't foreshadowing a conflict-plagued future marriage.

On the contrary, I explained that we were going to have a *"grrreeat"* marriage. "Remember," I said, "I'm the son of world-renowned marriage expert Dr. Gary Smalley. Certainly something has rubbed off during the twenty-three years I've spent under his roof! Besides, I'm almost halfway through my master's degree—in marriage and family counseling. And I'm out once a month speaking at marriage conferences with my dad. I think it's safe to say that I know a little more than the average guy on how to have a successful marriage!"

Can you believe after *that* impressive relational résumé, Erin still didn't seem persuaded?

"Trust me." I begged with my best pouty face.

Let me make this very simple: Erin was right and I was wrong. As a matter of fact, I was very wrong!

Once Erin and I were married, we managed our relational conflict poorly. It got so bad that two years into our marriage I was convinced that we were one more argument away from Erin's leaving.

And then *the* argument happened. We had gotten into this huge fight while I was driving. We were yelling at each other, and our argument had escalated to the point that I was so mad I had to get off the road. I pulled into a parking lot in front of a health club. We didn't consider the fact that our windows were down or what we must have looked like.

Erin was nine-and-a-half months pregnant with her big ol' tummy, and we were in the midst of spouting off horrible things to each other when a woman came out of the health club. Apparently someone had dropped a membership card on the ground near our car, and when the woman saw it she picked it up to hand to Erin, assuming it was hers.

Prior to the lady's arriving by the side of the car, Erin had given me a scathing comeback and told me that she was just about ready to get out of the car. So just then, I yelled at her, "Fine, just walk home!" Apparently this lady heard me. She took one look at my pregnant wife and, absolutely appalled at my inhumane statement, literally tried to help Erin out of the car. The woman tried to comfort Erin by saying, "It's okay. I'll help you get somewhere safe!"

If only I had kept a copy of my relational résumé in the car, I could have given it to the lady to help her realize that I wasn't a complete jerk.

I'll never forget that woman's look of total disgust. That was the lowest point in my marriage. I was convinced in that moment that my wife and I were not going to make it. What had gone wrong? We'd been so in love with each other before we'd gotten married. Although we struggled like other couples that first year, I never thought we'd get to this point.

The good news is that Erin and I made it. Actually, we didn't just survive those early years, but we actually thrived.

You might be wondering how in the world we went from a strange woman trying to pry my pregnant wife out of the car to thriving. Sure, we did many of the traditional things like counseling, joining a marriage small group, and getting mentored by a healthy older couple, Dr. Gary and Carrie Oliver. But as I look back over the past seventeen years, one thing really stands out as the key.

To understand what changed our marriage, we must go back to what Christ called the greatest of all the commandments.

THE GREATEST COMMANDMENT

Most of us have heard the story of what happened one time when Jesus was engaged in a public debate with the Pharisees and Sadducees:

> One of the teachers of the law came and heard them debating. Noticing that Jesus had given them a good answer, he asked him, "Of all the commandments, which is the most important?"
>
> "The most important one," answered Jesus, "is this: 'Hear, O Israel, the Lord our God, the Lord is one. Love the Lord your God with all your heart and with all your soul and with all your mind and with all your strength.' The second is this: 'Love your neighbor as yourself.' There is no commandment greater than these." (Mark 12:28–31)

The part I want to focus on is the word *love*. Here we are commanded to love God and to love others as we love ourselves. That's a lot of loving! But here's the thing: everything I thought I knew about love was wrong. Or at least there is one key part of love that I completely misunderstood. And unfortunately, Erin and I had to learn it the hard way.

The truth is that I thought I understood love. After all, it's one of the most commonly used words in our vocabulary. Think about how often we use the term *love* in our communication. We use *love* to express a great liking for someone ("I love my wife") or something ("I love peanut butter Cap'n Crunch"). We use *love* to communicate the pleasure we get from something ("I love cooking" and "I love golf"). We use *love* to convey a strong positive emotion of regard ("He loves his work").

We express our devotion through the word *love* ("The theater was her first love"). The word *beloved* means a person who is greatly loved or who is dear to the heart. *Love* can verbalize a deep feeling of sexual desire and attraction ("He is madly in love with her"). *Love* can represent the score of zero in tennis or squash ("It was 40-love"). There's even a song that sings about loving love ("I love loving you").

The Bible actually started this entire trend because the word *love* is used 697 times in the Bible.[1]

Speaking of the Bible, there are some powerful verses about love. One of my favorites is 1 Corinthians 13:1:

> If I speak in the tongues of men and of angels, but have not love, I am only a resounding gong or a clanging cymbal. If I have the gift of prophecy and can fathom all mysteries and all knowledge, and if I have a faith that can move mountains, but have not love, I am nothing. If I give all I possess to the poor and surrender my body to the flames, but have not love, I gain nothing.

Erin and I had this love passage read in our wedding ceremony:

> Love is patient, love is kind. It does not envy, it does not boast, it is not proud. It is not rude, it is not self-seeking, it is not easily angered, it keeps no record of wrongs. Love does not delight in evil but rejoices with the truth. It always protects, always trusts, always hopes, always perseveres.
>
> Love never fails. (1 Corinthians 13:4–8)

Love truly makes the world go 'round!

All that to say that *love* is a very complicated word. No wonder I was confused about love.

At this point, you might be wondering exactly what was confusing. The answer is found in not what happened when Erin and I were doing well relationally, but during the times when we were hurt, angry, and frustrated with each other. You see, love is easy when things are going great. On the other hand, love can be tough when things are difficult between you and your spouse.

When Erin and I got married, I just assumed that we would always be "in love" with each other. I never thought things would be perfect, but I certainly didn't think I would have moments when I really didn't feel love toward Erin. If I were to be completely honest, that day in the car when we were fighting and the woman tried to help Erin out of the car, I didn't feel love toward her in that moment.

It's like the Righteous Brothers' song, "You've Lost That Lovin' Feelin'." There have been hours and even days when I'd lost that loving feeling—that I didn't feel any love toward Erin.

What was difficult about this is that I wasn't sure what it meant. Did the absence of the feeling of love mean that there was something wrong with me? Was it Erin? Perhaps the problem was with our marriage. Maybe we weren't supposed to be married, that Erin wasn't my soul mate, that there was some poor woman roaming the world looking for me, but I wasn't available.

Sounds crazy, huh? Listen to these stories about not feeling love that couples posted on the Internet.

♡ I've been married for almost twenty years. For the last ten years we have been sleeping in separate rooms. My husband is not affectionate with me, he does not tell me he loves me or that I look nice or say anything endearing to me. He never was real affectionate in our marriage, but it's like we have our own separate lives now. I've already told my husband that I don't feel love for him anymore, but I am afraid I'll end up with nothing if I am the one who leaves.

♡ When I'm down, my wife is the only person I can be with and feel no aversion for. But I don't feel love for her. I know intellectually that I love her, but I can't feel it.

♡ My husband and I have been married less than one year. This weekend was a hard one for me. I think I cried every day. I'm just having such a hard time in our marriage right now. I'm just so discouraged. I get mad at my husband over nothing quite often. And I don't feel love for him a lot of the time, which burdens my heart with sorrow.

♡ I have been married for about nine months. My wife is relatively good looking and caring. However, for some reason I don't feel attracted to her, and I don't feel love for my wife either. Please help!

♡ I have been with my husband for fifteen years now. Though I am committed to this marriage and to my duties as a wife and mother, and I am not contemplating divorce, I don't feel love for him and don't feel physical desire for him. Frankly, I don't find him to be a lovable person. And because I feel so terribly overburdened with responsibilities of supplementing our income, housekeeping, and parenting, I have strong feelings of resentment that get in the way of any desire for intimacy with him. I can't bear to kiss him and kind of have to

27

work up a mental fantasy to engage in physical intimacy. Is it possible to awaken feelings of love for him in my heart?

♡ I know this is a cruel thing to say, but I have lost all love for my wife. I appreciate that she is a very good mom to my children, but how do I break it to her so she will understand that her husband no longer loves her. This even hurts me to say it, but it's true. Should I continue to pretend I love her, as I did marry her twelve years ago and had two beautiful children with her? Should I wait till the kids grow older and then ask for a divorce? Should I stay or should I go? They say honesty and being open is key to successful marriages, but how can I do this without breaking her heart?

♡ I have now left my husband after forty years of marriage. I have steadily realized that I was living a lie, I didn't want to be around him, be near him, hear him tell me he loved me as I didn't know what to reply, I didn't love him. It ate away at me, making me ill and unhealthy and sad, and I knew I had to leave. I know I have done everything to try to make things right, but when love is gone, the purpose of your life vanishes. I am now looking for a new purpose after all these years, nearly a lifetime.

♡ My husband of twenty years had an affair. Since discovery two years ago we have made major changes in our lives (jobs, cities) in attempts for reconciliation. Some days I feel love for him, and other days the betrayal is too great to ever seemingly get past (today is one of those days). He, too,

is putting forth great efforts toward our future together. I think I do still love him, but I also think
the lies and betrayal have killed my ability to feel
any type of love toward him.

What about you? Have there been times when you didn't feel
love toward your spouse? I'm sure if you're honest that there
have been moments or even seasons like this. Perhaps you feel
that way right now.

When I experienced those lonely, empty feelings, the only
thing I was certain about was that I needed to do something to
bring back the love. I thought there was something I could do to
rekindle or ignite the love I wasn't feeling.

However, this is where I went wrong. This is the part of love
that I didn't understand. As a matter of fact, it is the most common question I hear from couples who come in for marriage
counseling: *"Can you help us feel in love again?"* The question can
take many forms:

♡ Is it possible to awaken feelings of love in my heart
   for my husband?
♡ Can you help me feel love again for my wife?
♡ How can I restore the love in my marriage again?
♡ Is it too late to rekindle our love?
♡ How can I bring healing and restoration of love
   and trust to my marriage?
♡ Can I ever love her again?
♡ Is it possible to rediscover the passion we once had
   for each other?
♡ Can you help me feel like something besides his
   roommate?

But in the end, they're all asking for the same miracle: *help us find that lovin' feelin' again!*

Erin and I were there too. I asked the counselor the same question: "I love her, but I'm not sure I'm 'in love' with her. Can you help?" I was so confused when we fought and doubted our love for each other, because the conflict was so painful. I remember putting so much pressure on myself to figure out how to generate love for Erin. Looking back, I wish someone had explained a very simple, relationship-changing concept to me. And it has everything to do with where love comes from.

WHERE DOES LOVE COME FROM?

In my work with couples when I hear the statement "I don't feel love for my spouse anymore," I just blow by it. *What?* you might be thinking, *How can you simply let that go? Isn't not feeling in love with your spouse a huge problem?*

It's not that I ignore the fact that someone does not feel love for his or her spouse. It's that I've come to recognize that I need to help this couple shift paradigms and look at their situation differently. Instead of discussing love, I usually ask them something that really gets them thinking. *Where does love come from?*

Love is not about chemistry or magic. Love cannot be generated. My inability to create love for Erin was not a sign that something was wrong with me, that Erin was unlovable, that our marriage was broken, or that she wasn't my soul mate (I hate that term!). It was simply a function of the reality that, as humans, no love originates with us.

God is the author, creator, and generator of love. Love comes from God and God is love (see 1 John 4:7–8)! As a matter of fact, the only reason we can love at all is because He first poured His love into us (see 1 John 4:19). The point is, all that love we talk about, write about, and sing about—none of it comes from us. We do not generate a single drop of love. It all comes from God.

By design, here is how the process of love works. When we open our hearts to God, we receive His love. He then fills our hearts abundantly full of His love (see Romans 10:10). Once our hearts are full of God's love, we then open our hearts and share love with others. His love passes through me from God to others. When I wholeheartedly engage God and my spouse, the flow of love is full and complete. This is how we live out the Greatest Commandment.

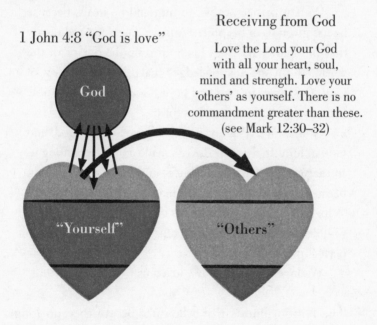

1 John 4:8 "God is love"

Receiving from God

Love the Lord your God with all your heart, soul, mind and strength. Love your 'others' as yourself. There is no commandment greater than these. (see Mark 12:30–32)

God

"Yourself"

"Others"

The key is to understand that the ultimate source of love is God. We cannot even love God until He fills our hearts with His love. The condition for loving others is *first* to experience God's own love. Consider 1 John 4:7–19:

Dear friends, let us love one another, for love comes from God. Everyone who loves has been born of God and knows God. Whoever does not love does not know God, because God is love. This is how God showed his love among us: He sent his one and only Son into the world that we might live through him. This is love: not that we loved God, but that he loved us and sent his Son as an atoning sacrifice for our sins. Dear friends, since God so loved us, we also ought to love one another. No one has ever seen God; but if we love one another, God lives in us and his love is made complete in us.

We know that we live in him and he in us, because he has given us of his Spirit. And we have seen and testify that the Father has sent his Son to be the Savior of the world. If anyone acknowledges that Jesus is the Son of God, God lives in him and he in God. And so we know and rely on the love God has for us.

God is love. Whoever lives in love lives in God, and God in him. In this way, love is made complete among us so that we will have confidence on the day of judgment, because in this world we are like him. There is no fear in love. But perfect love drives out fear, because fear has to do with punishment. The one who fears is not made perfect in love.

We love because he first loved us.

The bottom line is that when people say they no longer feel love for their spouses, the problem isn't love. God is love, and His love is always available. God's love is like air—it's all around. You don't have to be Christian for God's love to flow through you. God's love flows through you when you open your heart.

If love isn't the issue, what's the real problem when people don't feel love toward each other? Let me explain by telling you about my daughter's first day of kindergarten.

THE STATE OF YOUR HEART

I will never forget my daughter Taylor's first day of kindergarten. Erin and I stood on the corner of our street waving as Taylor's bus drove off with our little girl. Erin was weeping, and I had to get her into the house before the neighbors started to think I was doing something to her. (Remember, I have a history of people misunderstanding why Erin is crying!)

After school, Erin was away, so I got to welcome Taylor home from her first day by myself. I was standing on the front porch waiting for my precious daughter when I saw the bus pull up. I was so excited to hear all about her first day. When the bus finally stopped and all the kids jumped out, I was shocked by what I saw. It took a few seconds for it to sink in, but I finally focused on what it was—Taylor was holding hands with a boy!

I'm sure my jaw hit the floor, because I think I choked on a bug. I couldn't believe it. My little girl was holding hands with a boy. *A boy!*

Instead of reacting, I gave Taylor the benefit of the doubt. *It must be a bus buddy*, I reasoned.

But as the other kids dispersed, not only did Taylor keep holding this kid's hand, but now they were running up the sidewalk, right toward me. Before I had time to process this nightmare, Taylor yelled out, "Hi, Dad! This is Hank, and we're in love. And we're going to get married!"

And with that bit of good news, I think I started to gag. At

33

least that's what it sounded like. After regaining my composure, and with the premarital couple standing before me, I thought I had to have a little bit of fun with them.

"So you guys are in love?" I asked.

"Uh huh."

"And you're going to get married?"

"Uh huh," they both said, nodding their heads.

"Being five and all," I said, holding back a smile, "where will you guys live?"

They looked at me, back to each other, and shrugged their shoulders, and then Taylor dragged Hank to the side of the porch so they could huddle up and discuss my question. I could barely make out what they were saying. Then in unison they turned, and Taylor said, "Dad, if it's okay with you and Mom, Hank and I would like to live out in the backyard, in the Little Tykes house" (one of those plastic houses for toddlers).

"Sure," I said, with a grin. "Mom will love having you so close. We can visit any time we want, like real in-laws do. Now, although you'll have a sweet place to live, you will need stuff to go into your house. I'd like to get you something special. We'll call it a housewarming gift. What kind of stuff will you need to survive our cold Missouri winters?"

Once again they looked at me, back to each other, and shrugged their shoulders, and this time they walked to the side of the porch together. As I watched them discuss their ideas, I thought that it wasn't a good sign when your five-year-old daughter and her fiancé problem solve better than you and your wife do, but that's a whole different book!

When they finished, my future son-in-law stepped up and said, "We decided that we need three things."

Wow, I thought, *they've simplified their lives to three things.*

"All right, lay it on me."

Hank stood straight and looked me in the eyes. "We need the TV and the remote" (that only counted as one thing apparently), "a roll of toilet paper, and a box of Lucky Charms."

As I thought about Hank's request, I realized that it made perfect sense. As a guy, I could live six months off those three things alone. So I high-fived him and welcomed him to the family.

Over the next several weeks, it was very strange watching my little girl relate to Hank. Actually it was kind of creepy how they always seemed to be together, laughing and playing.

And then *it* happened.

As I returned home from work one evening, I found Taylor weeping in her room. I quickly discovered that Hank had broken up with her. The engagement was officially off!

After I silently looked up toward the heavens and gave thanks, I comforted my daughter. I'll never forget what she said. As my precious Taylor lay on my arm, she looked at me and cried, "Daddy, I loved him so much."

I'm not sure, but I may have gagged again.

"But he hurt me so bad. I hate him now, and I want him to die!"

In case you were wondering, she gets that from Erin's side of the family.

I've often thought about that moment and what Taylor said. Not so much because I fear for my own safety if she gets mad at me, but because it's the same thing I've watched so many couples go through.

Isn't it interesting that earlier that same day, Taylor was in love with Hank (whatever that might mean to a five-year-old girl)? But then once she was hurt, not only did she not love him anymore, she wanted him dead. What happened in those twelve hours? The answer is the same thing that happened to me and Erin in the middle of our difficult years. It's the same thing that happens to any couple that goes through marriage problems and no longer feels love toward each other. What happened to Taylor? One thing: *her heart shut down toward Hank*. That's it.

A CLOSED HEART

When someone doesn't feel love toward one's spouse, I assume that someone has the door to his or her heart closed for some reason or another. But the problem is that people want to make the issue about love. "I'm just not in love with her anymore."

Remember, we are not the creators of love. God is love. No love comes from us! We love because God first loved us. The real issue is never love, because God's love is always available. Unfortunately, most couples don't understand this. All you have to do is look at the things that people usually cite as reasons for divorce:

- ♡ We're not compatible.
- ♡ Our differences are killing us.
- ♡ He had an extramarital affair.
- ♡ She has too many unrealistic expectations.
- ♡ We fight and argue constantly.
- ♡ We have nothing in common.
- ♡ I can't stand his personality quirks.
- ♡ We rarely have sex.
- ♡ All he does is work.
- ♡ We have no money.
- ♡ I feel like I'm living with a roommate.
- ♡ I finally found my "soul mate."
- ♡ Her parents are driving me crazy.

Certainly these issues exacerbate things, but I assert that these are secondary problems. The real issue is that hearts have closed to each other. Let me say that again. In relationships, the real issue isn't love; the issue is the state of your heart—is it *open* or *closed*?

I find this in most every hurting couple I've worked with: they have shut down. They are completely disconnected from each other. People often use other words to describe a dead heart: detached, indifferent, numb, lifeless, heartless, alone, emotionally unavailable, or hard-hearted.

Do you feel that way? Do others accuse you of being this way? It's like what the Tin Woodman said in *The Wizard of Oz:*

It was a terrible thing to undergo, but during the year I stood there I had time to think that the greatest loss I had known was the loss of my heart. While I was in love I was the happiest man on earth; but no one can love who has not a heart, and so I am resolved to ask Oz to give me one.

Here is the real problem. When my heart shuts down to someone, especially to my spouse, then God's love is no longer flowing through me to her. This is why people say they don't feel "in love." If my heart is closed, then I have shut God's love out. This is what is actually happening when people do not feel love for their spouses. They have simply closed their hearts to their mates, for good reasons I'm sure.

Jesus said: "Moses permitted you to divorce your wives because your *hearts were hard.* But it was not this way from the beginning" (Matthew 19:8).

This idea has been extremely freeing to me. Instead of putting my efforts and energies into doing something we have zero

A Closed Heart

1 John 4:8 "God is love"

"For this people's heart has become cal-
loused; they hardly hear with their ears,
and they have closed thier eyes. Otherwise they might see with their eyes, hear
with their ears, understand with their
hearts and turn, and I would heal them."
(Acts 28:27)

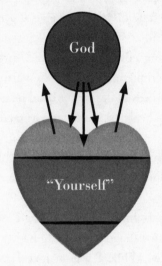

ability to do (i.e., create love), I now focus on the condition of my
heart: is it open or closed? Because if I have closed my heart to
my spouse, then I have closed it to God as well. This is how we
become the biggest barrier in living out the Greatest Commandment. When my heart is closed, I don't get filled up with God's
love; therefore, I don't have anything to give out. I can't love
God, myself, or others.

Obviously, God will continue to love me and others—He
doesn't need me to fulfill His purposes. But He wants me to be
a part of the process. I receive so much when God uses me to
love others: patience, kindness, encouragement, pride, polite-
ness, selflessness, self-control, forgiveness, rejoicing with the
truth, protection, trust, hope, and perseverance (see 1 Corinthians 13:4–7).

The good news is that we have a choice. We have control
over our hearts. God created us with the capacity to choose. We

can't always choose our relationships—we didn't choose our parents or our siblings or our children—but we *can* choose who we open our hearts to.

First and foremost, we get to choose if we want a relationship with Christ. "Here I am! I stand at the door and knock. If anyone hears my voice and opens the door, I will come in and eat with him, and he with me" (Revelation 3:20).

What "door" do you think He's knocking on? The door of your heart. You see, Christ is a gentleman. He doesn't break down the door of your heart. Instead, He knocks and then waits patiently. You choose who you open your heart to, and you choose when you close it down. No one shuts your heart down. People may do things that lead you to react to their actions by shutting down. But it's still your choice. That's great news. It's your choice.

If your heart is closed right now, let that be okay. I'm not trying to convince you to open your heart to anyone. If your heart is closed, we're sure it's closed for good reasons. I just want you to move forward understanding this truth. I want you to embrace what is really going on—your heart may be closed to some degree. In the end, if you desire intimacy with your spouse, it will require an open heart. This book can give you the tools to have a heart that is fully open and fully available to God and others, especially to your spouse.

Before we move on, let's define the heart.

WHAT IS THE HEART?

Several years ago I asked hundreds of married couples to define the heart. Here are some of my favorite responses:

The heart is . . .

- ♡ The wellspring of life
- ♡ A reflection of the true self
- ♡ The core of a person
- ♡ The deep center of one's life
- ♡ The innermost part of the human personality
- ♡ Me
- ♡ The place we connect to God and others
- ♡ The essence of who we are
- ♡ The source of our real character

According to Dallas Willard, the heart is the executive center of a human life. The heart is where decisions and choices are made for the whole person.[2]

My favorite definition of the heart is that it is *the vital center of the real you.*

Another way to look at the heart is through the analogy of the Holy of Holies. In the Holy Place of the tabernacle and the temple there was an inner room called the Holy of Holies, or the Most Holy Place. Judging from its name, we can see that it was a most sacred room, a place no ordinary person could enter. It was considered God's special dwelling place in the midst of His people.

Whoever entered into the Holy of Holies was coming into the very presence of God. In fact, anyone except the high priest who entered the Holy of Holies would die. Even the high priest, God's chosen mediator for His people, could pass through the veil and enter this sacred dwelling only once a year, on a prescribed day called the Day of Atonement.

Even then, the high priest had to make some meticulous preparations. He had to wash himself, put on special clothing, bring burning incense to let the smoke cover his eyes from a direct view of God, and bring blood with him to make atonement for sins.[3] It has been said that the high priest had a rope tied around his ankle whenever he entered the Holy of Holies. If the high priest had not properly prepared according to divine instructions, God might kill him. With the rope tied to him and the other end of the rope leading outside the Holy of Holies, his body could be dragged out. How would you like a rope tied around your ankle as part of your regular work attire?

This is how sacred and precious the Holy of Holies was. Our hearts are just as sacred, just as precious. And yet do we treat our hearts like the Israelites treated the Holy of Holies? No. Many people ignore, reject, abandon, judge, abuse, and are careless with their hearts. Our hearts are the most valuable part of who we are.

THE IMPORTANCE OF THE HEART

My son, Garrison, understands how important his little heart is. And whenever I think about my son and his precious heart, I smile at what happened on our first father-son road trip.

When Garrison was four years old, I had the opportunity to speak to some college coaches at the Final Four basketball tournament. The games were being played in Indianapolis that year, which was only about a ten-hour drive from our home, so I thought it would be perfect for a road trip.

Garrison and I had an amazing time watching the games, buying souvenirs, and stuffing our faces with hot dogs and snacks. We even had a tornado touch down in downtown Indianapolis while we were there. It was a real guys' trip. To top off the perfect experience, Garrison gave me a big hug and said, "You're the best daddy in the whole wide world." I was in heaven!

The next morning, we started the ten-hour drive back to

Northwest Arkansas. We had been in the car no more than five minutes when Garrison announced, "I have to go really bad."

"Can't you hold it?"

"I'm going to go in my pants if you don't stop!"

Since I had recently promised Erin that I would no longer stop on the side of the road so he could go, I shot back, "You're going to have to wait for a gas station."

Clearly Garrison had been praying and had had his quiet time that morning, because around the next corner we found a truck stop.

In the men's room there were four urinals, with truckers taking up two of the spots. Most women don't know that guys have several unspoken rules when using the urinals, with the most important one being "No Talking." Every guy knows this. It has been passed down from father to son for generations. But apparently I had somehow inadvertently broken the chain. Talk about a generational curse!

So there we were—me, Garrison, and the two truckers—when all of a sudden, Garrison shouts out, "Hey, Dad, look. I'm holding Jesus in my hand!"

I couldn't believe what I had just heard. There wasn't supposed to be any talking, much less blasphemous talk. I quickly looked up to the heavens and pleaded, "I swear I didn't teach him that. He's home all day with his mother!"

As the truckers laughed at my son (or maybe it was at me), I peered around the divider to silence any more wicked chitchat. It was then I noticed Garrison's "other" hand was over his heart.

"See, Dad, I'm holding Jesus."

And then it dawned on me. We had talked earlier about the fact that Jesus lives in our hearts. Praise the Lord! I wasn't a complete failure as a father, and Garrison wasn't going to be struck down by lightning.

I love that Garrison gets the importance of his little heart. Growing up, I never gave my heart a second thought. I was more interested in thinking my way through life. I had no idea how important the heart is. Here are just a few of many reasons why our hearts are extremely important:

God created an amazing organ within each of us. Weighing less than a pound, the human heart will beat about 2.5 billion times and pump 80 million gallons of blood in an average lifetime, a volume that is enough to fill more than three supertankers![4]

Our hearts are important to God so much so that He listed it first in the Greatest Commandment: "Love the Lord your God *with all your heart* and with all your soul and with all your mind and with all your strength." In this verse, God is describing the whole person (heart, soul, mind, and strength), but why did He reference the heart first? Coincidence? No way! God is not random in His dealings. He acts deliberately. His choices always have a purpose.

The heart is one of the most central themes in the Scripture. The word *heart* appears in no fewer than 926 references in the Bible.[5] The Bible addresses the heart more than any other topic—more than how we think, more than belief or obedience, more than money, more than works or service, and even more than worship. Maybe God is trying to tell us something![6]

Our faith originates in our hearts (see Romans 10:9-10), and the heart is the dwelling place of the Lord (see Ephesians 3:17)—just ask Garrison!

The heart contains our deepest desires (Psalm 21:2; 2 Chronicles 1:11; Romans 1:24), and these desires of our hearts will be granted when we delight in the Lord (Psalm 37:4).

The heart is the connection point between two people (1 Peter 1:22).

It is the source of creativity and courage (Joshua 2:11; 5:1).

The heart contains wisdom (1 Kings 3:9-12; Ecclesiastes 8:5) and uses that wisdom to teach us (Psalm 16:7).

Our deepest secrets are held in our hearts (Psalm 44:21; Job 31:33). The heart is the source of a "hidden man" that produces qualities of character (1 Peter 3:4).

One of the most interesting truths about the heart is that it can reason (Ecclesiastes 7:25; Mark 2:8) and that it has "thoughts and attitudes" (Hebrews 4:12). Literally, our deepest thinking is done in the heart: "For as he thinks in his heart, so is he" (Proverbs 23:7 NKJV). This is why Jesus, knowing our thoughts, asked, "Why are you *thinking these things in your hearts*?" (Luke 5:22). Biomedical research done by neurocardiologist Dr. J. Andrew Armour has validated what the Bible has been saying for thousands of years. Dr. Armour found that the heart is not just a simple pump but a highly complex, self-organized information-processing center with its own functional "brain." Did you know that your heart has brain cells (neurons)? We have as many brain cells in our hearts as we do in the lower parts of our brains. At least forty thousand neurons exist in the heart. But the neurons in your heart are more than five thousand times more powerful! With each beat, the heart continuously communicates with the brain and body via the nervous system, hormonal system, bioelectromagnetic interactions, and other pathways.[7]

It seems that the heart is inextricably intertwined with our whole human nature—influencing and being influenced by everything we do! It operates something like a network of spiritual connections that senses every thought and every emotion, both external and internal, and will feed back its own desire and focus, influencing and controlling our behavior more than we realize.

HOW HAVE WE MISSED THE IMPORTANCE OF THE HEART?

For years I've been asking the men at my marriage seminars to raise their hands if they were brought up in homes where their dads or significant male role models taught how important their hearts are in life and in their relationships. Never have I had more than 2 to 3 percent of the men raise their hands.

I then ask the women to raise their hands if they were brought up in homes where their moms or significant female role models taught them not just about their hearts but showed them how to take great care of their hearts. Again, never more than 3 to 4 percent of the women raised their hands.

Our hearts are so important—it seems so simple and the evidence is all around—but somehow most of us have missed this truth. What's going on here? I think John Eldredge summed it up best in his excellent book *Waking the Dead*:

> I find it almost hard to believe a case must be made that the heart is . . . well, at the heart of it all. Of life. Of each person. Of God. And of Christianity.
>
> It is diabolical, despicable, and is downright evil. This bears the mark of the enemy. The enemy knows how vital the heart is, even if we do not, and all his forces are fixed upon its destruction. For if he can disable or deaden your heart, then he has effectively foiled the plan of God, which was to create a world where love reigns.

By taking out your heart, the enemy takes out you, and you are essential to the Story. Once you begin to see with the eyes of your heart, once you have begun to know it is true from the bottom of your heart, it will change everything. The story of your life is the story of the long and brutal assault on your heart by the one who knows what you and your marriage could be and fears it.[8]

WHY DO YOU NEED AN OPEN HEART?

In order for intimacy and deep connection to occur, your heart must be open to God and others. You want to love your spouse the way Peter calls us to in 1 Peter 1:22: "Love one another deeply, from the heart." To that, you must discover why the door to your heart is closed. And, then, you must discover how to get your heart back open.

Take a moment right now to evaluate where your heart is in your marriage. Is it shut down completely? Is it fully open?

Completely Closed   Completely Open

Wherever your heart is at this point in time, don't judge yourself, don't try to pry yourself open or remain oblivious any longer. Just let it be okay to be where you are today.

In the long term, though, your heart must be open if you want the wholehearted love God desires for you to have. Your heart is incredibly valuable, and our hope is that we can help you better understand how to keep your heart open and full of God's love so you can fully engage your heart in your marriage. This

kind of love without restraint will lead to the deepest level of intimacy, deeper than most of us could ever imagine.

Remember, above all else, guard your heart, because it's the
wellspring of life and relationships!

Next, let's explore how emotions are the voice of our hearts.
The key is to give our hearts a voice by being aware of our emotions and then managing our emotions in healthy ways.

Chapter 2
The Voice of the Heart

You are never a great man when you have more mind than heart.

—E. P. Beauchene

You cannot know what you cannot feel.

—Marya Mannes

"I THINK, THEREFORE I am."

This famous René Descartes quote has had the unfortunate effect of separating people into two parts: heart and mind, emotion and reason. As a result, the heart has been misunderstood, thought of as simply emotions ("She wears her heart on her sleeve") or passion ("He's got so much heart!"). The mind, then, is regarded as our seat of reason.

But we are much more than "thinking beings." We are *thinking and feeling* beings. Descartes got it wrong. What a distorted view of the human person![1]

The good news is that the heart is not just about emotions. This is why King Solomon (the wisest man who ever lived) asked for a wise and discerning heart and not for a massive brain: "Give your servant a *discerning heart* to govern your people and to distinguish between right and wrong. For who is able to govern this great people of yours?" (1 Kings 3:9).

John Eldredge, in *Waking the Dead*, explains why the heart is more than emotions:

> Yes, the heart is the source of our emotions. But we have equated the heart "with" emotion, and put it away for a messy and even dangerous guide. No doubt, many people have made a wreck of their lives following an emotion without stopping to consider whether it was a good idea to do so. Neither adultery nor murder is a rational act. But equating the heart with emotion is the same nonsense as saying that love is a feeling. . . . Emotions are the voice of the heart, to borrow Chip Dodd's phrase. Not the heart, but its voice. They express the deeper movements of the heart, as when we weep over the loss of someone we love, or when we cheer at the triumph of a son's team at the state championships. The mind stands detached, but it is with the heart that we experience and respond to life in all its fullness.[2]

As you can see, our emotions are the voice of the heart, but the heart is more than emotion.

Perhaps you're thinking, *What does it matter if I separate heart and mind? This sounds better suited for a philosophy class than a marriage book.* More than a philosophical debate, understanding this distinction is vital to a wholehearted marriage. If we don't value our emotions, we end up being disconnected from a huge part of our hearts. We become two-dimensional—more head than heart. On the other hand, if we overvalue our feelings, we end up being controlled by our emotions. We become emotionally reckless—more heart than head.

I wish I would have understood the importance of my heart and emotions. It would have saved me and my marriage much pain and anguish.

I FEEL FINE

"Greg just won't talk about his feelings!" Erin complained to Stacy, our counselor. "When I ask him how he feels, he just shuts down and refuses to talk about it, or he just says 'Fine'!"

So there I sat shifting nervously, awaiting the trip I was about to go on—a guilt trip, that is. Alternating my gaze between my wife and Stacy, I knew I was caught between a rock and hard place. Since Stacy was a woman, I just knew she was going to light me up! But I will never forget her response to Erin.

"Erin," Stacy said calmly, "have you ever thought about what happens to Greg when you ask him about his feelings? What seems like a perfectly natural question to a woman is a very different experience for a guy."

Stacy definitely had my attention. Erin's too.

"What seems like an innocent question to a woman is not so simple to the average man. And here's why. Women tend to get quiet when they feel hurt or lied to. Therefore, when Greg is quiet, you probably assume his silence indicates that he is upset or is lying."

"That's exactly right," Erin said. "When Greg doesn't want to share his feelings or says he's fine, I assume he is upset with me or that he is hiding something. It drives me crazy!"

"Although there are exceptions, most men stop communicating when they have a problem to solve. Their silence is not about deception or that they're upset. Instead, they've been conditioned all their lives to solve problems by using their brains and not their emotions. So asking him what he's thinking about is probably a more realistic question than asking him what he's feeling."

This woman was good. I smiled at Erin and said, "That's what I've been trying to tell you."

Stacy ignored me. "Erin, I'm sure you know that our American culture supports emotional expression for girls but discourages it for boys. Think about it. From Clint Eastwood to the Marlboro Man, from football heroes to fathers, males at a very young age are given many messages, both explicit and subtle, about manhood and emotions.

"They're told things like this: Real men don't cry. Get up and shake it off. No pain, no gain. Stand on your own feet and solve your own problems. Don't cry; be tough! Work hard; achieve high performance. Don't be a wuss! Be a man. A winner never quits, and a quitter never wins. Fear and vulnerability are for wimps. Play through the pain. Act rather than feel. A boy may cry but a man conceals his pain."

Wow, I thought. I'd never really considered how the things I'd heard from coaches, teachers, pastors, neighbors, friends' fathers, and TV images and movies were laced with these damaging messages.

Stacy continued. "Boys growing up in our culture learn to stifle their tears and other emotional displays. The message they receive is 'Push it down, stuff it inside, don't show that feeling, otherwise you will be seen as weak and as a failure.' Boys in many Westernized countries learn that in order to be 'a man' they should hide their feelings and silence their fears. Research shows that men, when compared with women, have an impaired ability to identify and express their emotions, have difficulty in expressing a range of emotions, and take longer to articulate their emotions.[3] Sadly, this restriction of emotional expression leaves men with a limited range of emotional tools to manage relationships, conflict, adversity, and change."

Erin reached over and took my hand. And for the first time in a long time, I felt understood. But I also felt exposed and very uncomfortable. It was like someone was shining a light into a very dark corner of my heart.

"Erin," Stacy said, "remember when you said that Greg says 'fine' to your question about his feelings? Do you know what 'fine' stands for: Feelings Inside Not Expressed."

Erin and I both laughed out loud, because it was so true. Great, now I could never use *fine* again. Thanks, Stacy!

"Since they have been taught to suppress their feelings, many men simply do not have the words to describe their emotions. And as you've experienced, this leads to great frustration in a marriage when one person cannot express his needs, fears, hurt, and frustration. Men often feel overwhelmed by their wives when it comes to discussing emotional issues, because they cannot articulate their feelings. This leaves the average man feeling confused, angry, and helpless.

"As a result," Stacy said, "the average man has developed two primary responses to emotional issues. For vulnerable feelings including fear, hurt, and shame, men typically use anger as the 'manly' reaction. For nurturing feelings, including caring, warmth, connectedness, and intimacy, men channel these feelings through sex."[4]

Now I was really uncomfortable. *Why not just expose all of my deep secrets while you're at it, Doc?* I wanted to yell.

"Greg and Erin," Stacy said, "the truth is, we all have feelings—including men. The problem is that because of cultural messages, expectations, and traditions, most men have a difficult time noticing and understanding their emotions. For example,

Greg, think about some husbands you watch on TV. Who comes to mind?"

I thought about it for a few seconds. "How about Ray Barone from *Everybody Loves Raymond* and Doug Heffernan from *King of Queens*?"

"Perfect," Stacy said smiling. "Now think about how these men are portrayed. Are they depicted as strong, nurturing, and emotionally intelligent husbands or bumbling, dim-witted, and insensitive husbands whose emotional expression is usually limited to lust and anger?"

She made a good point.

"Despite Hollywood's depiction of men," Stacy said emphatically, "men *are* emotional. Erin, I know it may seem like Greg's emotions are in deep cryogenic suspension most of the time, but his emotions are there. He has the same capacity as you to experience the full range of emotions."

I instantly felt a sharp elbow pierce my side. "I knew it," Erin joked.

"The absence of emotions is not the problem," Stacy explained. "The real issue is that husbands and wives typically handle emotions very differently. A male's brain is wired for action during high emotion, whereas a woman's brain is wired for talking things over. When upset, women are likely to express their feelings directly and seek the support of friends and family, whereas a man's first instinct is to withdraw and hide his emotions—to go into the cave.

"And to make matters worse, when some husbands do begin to be more emotionally open and vulnerable at home, they often receive a very confusing message from their wives that says, 'Although I'm glad you're opening up, when you share your emotions and weaknesses, I get scared.'"

Erin jumped in immediately. "I know exactly what you're

talking about. There's a part of me that's thrilled when Greg shares his deepest feelings, but there's another part that gets freaked out. It's not that I don't like his getting emotional. I think it scares me that he may not be strong enough to take care of me and the kids. Is that weird?"

"It's not weird at all," Stacy said. "Unfortunately, most men interpret this mixed message as rejection or failure, and they stop being emotionally vulnerable."

"I remember sitting at the funeral for Erin's mother," I said. "During the viewing, we were sitting as a family. I had our son, Garrison, who was six at the time, in my lap. At one point he turned around and saw that I had tears in my eyes. He leaned in and whispered, 'Stop crying!' I think in his own way he was trying to say that real men don't cry. I think we constantly receive these subtle and sometimes very obvious messages that we are not supposed to have feelings."

"And sadly, the real loss you have suffered, Greg, is the loss of your heart."

Stacy let her words sink in and then turned to Erin.

"Erin, before you get too confident in your emotional abilities, understand that women are not always emotional experts. Although the perception in our culture is that women are more emotional than men and are supposed to be experts on emotions, this is far from the truth. Women may be naturally more aware of their emotions. They may experience a wider, more intense range of emotions. They may be more able to identify with and feel others' pain and be more emotionally expressive than men, but it doesn't mean they express emotions in healthy ways.[5]

"God did not design women to be more emotional or to have different emotions from men," Stacy said. "Many women find it difficult to make their feelings known and end up suppressing their emotions as well as any man. Take anger, for example. Unlike the many stereotypes involving women, we do not always easily express our anger. Many of us keep it stuffed down deep inside, while others may deal with it through passive aggressiveness, or even by targeting vulnerable and innocent people like children or the unknown individual driving next to us."[6]

"I think husbands need to be on that list," I quickly added.

"Although it's true that most women—notice I said 'most women'—seem to be more aware of their emotions and are more likely to verbalize their feelings, the problem is in how women manage their emotions. It would be a gross misconception to say that all women do a great job processing their emotions in healthy ways. This is far from reality."

Now it was Erin's turn to squirm in her seat.

Stacy stayed focused on Erin. "What I've noticed in my clinical work with women and in my own life is that we view feelings as facts. Whereas boys are taught to 'think' their way through life, causing so many of their decisions to feel heartless, girls are taught to 'feel' their way through life, making so many of their decisions appear unpredictable, emotionally reckless, and without thought.

"This is where we came up with expressions like these to describe women: emotional, drama queen, extremely talkative, overly sensitive, be careful or she'll have a cow, it's just that time of the month, emotionally out of control, histrionic, prima donna, she's just being emotional, irrational, hysterical, emotional tantrum, diva, she's having a hissy fit."

"Erin," Stacy said, "have you ever heard one of these stereotypes made in reference to you?"

Erin teared up as she talked about being called "overly sensitive" and "emotionally out of control" as a young girl.

I cringed as I thought about the messages I'd sent Erin about her feelings:

- ♡ Your feelings are wrong!
- ♡ You shouldn't feel that way!
- ♡ Why do you get so emotional?
- ♡ Calm down; it's just your monthly female time that's making you feel that way!
- ♡ That's not how you really feel!
- ♡ You're crazy!

Stacy continued, "Whereas boys are taught that real men don't cry, girls are taught to follow their emotions with reckless abandon. This is a huge problem for you both."

Erin and I just smiled at each other.

"Greg," Stacy said, "you seem to exist in your head, trying to think your way through life. Listening to you talk, you appear to react without paying hardly any attention to your feelings. You seem to place a greater importance on your mind and often ignore your emotions. Is this accurate?"

"I guess this is why we pay you the big bucks," I joked. But this was no laughing matter. "Seriously, I *think* you're right on the money. The truth is that there have been many times when Erin has accused me of being emotionally dead and numb inside. She said it was like my feelings have been frozen. Of course, I usually dismiss her, like shooing away a gnat. I hate to admit it, but I think she was right. In many ways I feel like the kid in that movie *Pleasantville*. It's a great movie about this lonely teenager who flees reality by watching *Pleasantville*—a 1950s black-and-white sitcom. It's kind of a cross between *Leave It to Beaver* and *Father Knows Best*.

"Ultimately, the boy and his twin sister are magically transported into Pleasantville, where they become Bud and Mary Sue Parker, two seemingly perfect teens with Ward-and-June Cleaver–esque parents. The interesting part of the movie is that Pleasantville is in black-and-white; there is no color. But when real people are introduced into this perfect, monochrome world and disrupt the lives of the Pleasantville citizens, vibrant colors start to appear. Gradually, more people and things turn multicolor, so that by the end of the movie, Pleasantville is no longer in black-and-white—it's in full color!

"That's me," I stated with passion. "I'm Pleasantville when it was in black-and-white. For most of my life I have tuned out emotions. I never really understood my own emotions, much less the emotions of others—especially Erin's. I've functioned in the objective world of facts, solutions, logic, and ideas. And I've avoided the subjective world of emotions and feelings, thinking these were irritating distractions that I needed to quickly get beyond."

"Sadly, Greg," Stacy said, "the more you sealed yourself off from your emotions, the more isolated and disconnected from your heart you've become. While you can suppress and repress your feelings, you cannot get rid of them. You always bury emotions alive. At some point they will always come out, but then they usually come exploding out like a volcanic eruption. Have you ever unexpectedly blown up at someone or thought 'Where did all *that* come from?'"

I didn't even have to look at Erin to sense her head nodding violently up and down.

"Greg, the only way to make peace with an unpleasant emotion is to face it, explore it, and understand it. Suppression takes an incredible amount of energy, energy that is constantly being tapped to maintain a wall of protection around your heart. This has robbed you of vital energy that could have been used for so many other important things.

"I'm sure that your habit of stuffing your emotions has made it difficult to connect well with others. Emotions are essential for a deep connection. You and Erin got acquainted by sharing facts, ideas, and opinions. Information has certainly deepened your knowledge about Erin, but it isn't the same as truly knowing her. Intimacy requires that you both open your hearts and share your desires, hopes, insecurities, and fears—your deepest emotions.

"By ignoring your emotions, your heart has been taken captive, and you've become emotionally immobile. It's like your feelings have atrophied—this is a wasting away of a part of the body because of poor nourishment and a lack of exercise. It's like the old saying 'If you don't use it, you'll lose it.' Ultimately, like in the movie, the heart and emotions are central in giving color to life."

I so badly wanted to defend myself, to explain that I'd never been trained to identify my emotions or to communicate my feelings, but I realized that she was right. My life did feel black-and-white. It was like I was living in monochrome and what I really wanted was color. I knew I needed my feelings to come back into balance—to be part of the equation.

I think Stacy knew she had pierced through the darkness that surrounded my heart and that I needed some time to absorb her words.

"Erin, while Greg lives in a black-and-white world, you live in high definition, 1080p [progressively scanned lines] color! While Greg ignores his emotions, you seem to be controlled by your emotions. Like a piece of wood floating in the ocean, you're at the mercy of your feelings—driven back and forth by the waves, often smashing against the rocks.

"When people are more heart than head, they appear to live their lives with the attitude 'If I feel it, it must be true.' Feelings or gut instinct become the standard for making decisions. To them, feelings equal facts and are valid simply because they experience them. They seem to believe that if they feel it, there's no possibility of being wrong, thus there's no need to check it out. Does this describe you, Erin?"

"It sure feels like me," Erin said, smiling. "No pun intended."

I even jumped into the mix. "Yes, when I try to reason with her, she usually accuses me of not understanding or validating her feelings."

"I do constantly feel misunderstood and invalidated," Erin said.

"Exactly," Stacy said, "the problem is feelings don't always equal facts. Because you feel something doesn't necessarily mean it is true. In order to bring balance to our lives, our emotions need our brains, and our brains need our emotions. This is how God designed the system to work. Otherwise we cannot live wholeheartedly. If it is all about the mind, we appear insensitive, uncaring, cold, and heartless. In contrast, if the measuring stick is emotions, we appear overly sensitive, dramatic, overwhelmed, and mindless. Does this make sense?"

We both nodded.

"In a marriage," Stacy said, looking at both of us, "when there is an imbalance in head versus heart, each spouse overcompensates and resents it. One will overfeel and the other will overthink. Thus, the feeler feels out of control emotionally, and the thinker feels lifeless."

That was the epiphany Erin and I had been searching for. Stacy's words perfectly described our marriage. I was the thinker and Erin was the feeler. And we both had built up a tremendous amount of resentment for each other. We were both tired of these roles, and we desperately craved a more balanced marriage.

"So how do we change?" I begged.

"I knew it wouldn't be very long until Greg asked for the solution." Stacy smiled. Erin just rolled her eyes. Apparently, it takes me much longer to change than it does Erin.

That's how it went for Erin and me as we sat in Stacy's office. What about you? How do you function in life and in your marriage? Do you focus more on the head or the heart? Do you tend to value one over the other? Would your spouse say that you are more of a head person or a heart person? It is impossible to have a wholehearted marriage when you are intellectually or emotionally out of balance.

Stacy finished our time together that day by encouraging us to start at the very beginning. Looking right at me, she asked, "What is an emotion?"

I had no idea!

WHAT ARE EMOTIONS?

Emotions are very complex. They're both mysterious and mystifying. The term has no single universally accepted definition—which is why most of us cannot even define it. Even the experts are unsure of what causes us to experience emotions.

The first thing about understanding emotions is to recognize that God created them. All of them. Let us never forget that we were created in God's image (Genesis 1:26). A key part of God is that He is emotional. Throughout Scripture we read about the emotions of God. God is loving (Psalm 144:2), jealous (Exodus 34:14), kind (Isaiah 54:8), angry (Deuteronomy 32:21), and patient (Romans 9:22), to name a few. Thus, emotions are God-given—we have emotions because God has emotions.

Not only did God create our emotions, but He made the heart the source of our emotions. In his book, *The Voice of the Heart*, Chip Dodd explains this perfectly:

> Feelings are the voice of the heart, and you will not have fullness until you're adept at hearing and experiencing all of them. When you are not aware of your feelings, your life is lived incompletely. Whenever you don't feel, you are blocked from living life to the fullest. Wherever you lack awareness of your heart, no room exists for God.[7]

The heart expresses itself through a wide range of emotions. According to Scripture our hearts can experience many positive things, such as joy, gladness, cheerfulness, merriment, steadfastness, wisdom, valor, purity, nobility, creativity, courage, conviction, faithfulness, hopefulness, and love. Our hearts can also feel many troublesome things, such as anger, anguish, fear, woundedness, sadness, grief, brokenness, division, foolishness, fright, faintheartedness, cowardice, forgetfulness, dullness, hate, stubbornness, sorrow, pride, hardness, wickedness, and perversion.

Many popular expressions in English describe the connection between emotions and the heart, such as *following one's heart*, being *kindhearted*, and *keeping a light heart*, as well as being *heartsick*, having a *heart of stone*, being *heart-stricken*, and *having a broken heart*.

So what is emotion? We can define an emotion as arising spontaneously rather than through conscious effort, as a reaction to an event that involves mental, behavioral, and physiological changes that motivate a person toward action (freeze, fight, or flight).[8] Thus, emotion can be viewed as a type of rapid, automatic calculation that triggers actions. These actions can be divided into four different elements:

♡ Emotions affect our *thoughts*. When you feel hurt by your spouse, you typically develop negative thoughts and beliefs about him or her. When you are flooded by emotion, it becomes almost impossible to have rational thoughts or to make wise decisions.

♡ Emotions prompt us to *react*. In the presence of an angry spouse, the rising fear may result in your shutting down (freeze), determining an escape route (flight), or yelling back (fight).

♡ Emotions impact us *physiologically* (respiratory, cardiovascular, and hormonal). For example, the increased heartbeat and perspiration that accompany fear, the warm sensation of a loved one's touch, the freezing response in the presence of a snake, butterflies in your stomach before a presentation, or the extra muscle tension that accompanies anger.

♡ Emotions inspire responses from *others*. "Emotions are contagious," wrote the Swiss psychiatrist Carl Jung.[9] The transmission of moods happens within milliseconds, so quickly that you can't control it, and so subtly that you're not really aware it's going on. Remember the old cliché "If Mom isn't happy, no one is happy!" Children read our feelings and mirror our emotions. They will soak up reassurance or fear, love or hate, safety or danger.

Our emotions influence virtually every aspect of our lives, including the social, mental, physical, and spiritual components. Dorothy Finkelhor, author of *How to Make Your Emotions Work for You*, says that emotions are:

> the motivating forces of our lives, driving us to go ahead, pushing us backward, stopping us completely, determining what we do, how we feel, what we want, and whether we get what we want. Our hates, loves, fears, and what to do about them are determined by our emotional structure. There is nothing in our lives that does not have the emotional factor as its mainspring. It gives us power or makes us weak, operates for our benefit or to our detriment, for our happiness or confusion.[10]

The real question remains: how do we live "wholeheartedly" and bring balance to our intellect and to our emotions?

BALANCING THE HEAD AND THE HEART

Christians are conflicted when it comes to emotions. Many evangelicals seem to have a love/hate relationship with emotions, no pun intended. Some see emotions as the essence of true religion. It's as if they live life through the Debby Boone song, "You Light Up My Life," specifically when she wonders how something could be wrong if it feels so deeply right.

Others consider emotions as unnecessary to authentic Christian living. The mind matters most. The emotions are simply the "caboose" on the train. They do nothing to actually keep the train moving and are thus disposable. They are enjoyable on occasion and in their proper place, but most of the time they are a bothersome nuisance.[11] These folks ignore their emotions by seeking logic, reason, and willpower. It's as if they live life through the song "Feelings," which says that feelings are insignificant and should be forgotten.

Christian psychologist Archibald Hart says that Christians often see emotions as incompatible with faith and experience great conflict trying to reconcile their experience of extreme feelings with their spirituality. This conflict is reinforced by a Christian culture that tends to resist expression of real feelings, because people fear being seen as a failure. Being honest about personal struggle will threaten their perceived respect from others. Attitudes and taboos about emotional expression lead to the following beliefs, Hart says:

- ♡ It is un-Christian to be depressed.
- ♡ To be an effective witness for Christ, I have to deny and conceal my feelings.
- ♡ If I give in to my emotions, I will lose control of myself.
- ♡ I should be free from emotional extremes. I should be calm at all times, neither too high nor too low.[12]

Put simply, on one side is the person who indulges his or her emotions, and on the other is the person who ignores his or her emotions. However, neither extreme is right. This is far from what God desires for our lives.

Remember, God made us to think. God created the mind, renews it in Christ, and uses it in the process of spiritual transformation. For this reason, the apostle Paul calls us to "be transformed by the renewing of your mind" (Romans 12:2). True spirituality is not irrationality. God calls us to love Him whole-heartedly—emotions, will, and mind. James Houston in *The Heart's Desire*, says:

> It is a scandal of our times that the mind and the emotions are in conflict, each separated from the other, and incapable of living meaningfully together, needing each other or recognizing their mutual dependence. An emotional life must be meaningful, and a rational existence must be clothed with appropriate emotions.[13]

God also made us to feel. God does not intend for us to be unfeeling people who are unaffected by the successes and tragedies of life. God certainly did not intend us to function by logic and reason alone! The inability to feel is not a strength but a weakness. As Gary Oliver explains in *Real Men Have Feelings Too*:

> The truth is that our emotions are God-given; they are a natural, healthy expression of our being made in his image. By God's design, our mind and emotions are intricately interrelated. Our choices influence what and how we feel. Our emotions influence how we interpret what we hear, what we think and the decisions that we make. Our thoughts or the mental interpretations we make of events around us influence how strongly we feel about something and thus the choices that we make. Our emotions and our mind are two different yet equally valuable ways of experiencing, understanding, and interpreting the world around us. They provide us with two different kinds of

information about ourselves and our world. They can balance each other. When our mind and emotions work together in harmony we are more likely to make wise and responsible choices.[14]

Thus, the key to living wholeheartedly is to bring balance to our intellect and emotions—to get our brains and feelings working together to make the best possible decisions.

The goal is to use feelings as information. You want the head to work with the heart. Honoring your feelings and emotions does not mean indulging in the feelings but honoring the data that the feelings contain and then using your mind to process the information like a computer:

> Heart = the data (information)
> Head = the processor (computer)

The best way to achieve this balance is by learning to recognize and understand your emotions (awareness) and to handle those emotions constructively (management). Let's take a look at these two components.

Awareness: Listening to the Voice of the Heart

If you tend to be more "head" than "heart," this section is for you.

You can't even begin to manage your emotions until you become aware of what they are. Just as you are aware of being hungry, needing to go to the bathroom, or having an itch at the small of your back, you must become aware of what you are feeling when you experience emotions.

Erin and I have worked hard to educate our children about life's dangers. We have taught them to identify things from poisonous snakes to poison ivy (we live in the Ozark Mountains of Arkansas). We have explained why we need to wash our hands with hand sanitizer instead of plain water. We have even taught them basic CPR and how to help someone who is choking. And we have definitely drilled into their heads the dangers of talking to strangers or accepting rides from people they don't know.

I remember one time in particular when we were teaching our middle daughter, Maddy, when she was about five years old, how to read labels to make sure she didn't eat something with peanuts in it (she has a mild peanut allergy). We had practiced ad nauseam until she could identify a peanut or any peanut derivative in her sleep.

Later that day an ice cream truck came into our neighborhood. Quickly our kids were begging Erin for money to buy their favorite ice cream treat. Because the truck was parked halfway down our block, Erin wanted to remind the girls of the dangers of talking to strangers.

"Maddy," Erin inquired, "what do you say if the ice cream man asks you to get in his truck?"

Maddy rolled her eyes. "We've been over this a million times, Mom. I'll tell him to give me something without peanuts."

The first step to understanding something is to become aware of it. Maddy wasn't yet aware of the danger posed by getting into a vehicle with a strange man, so she didn't sense the danger. But she would've certainly avoided anaphylactic shock!

Emotions provide us with information we need to stay safe in our world. It the reason emotions are so important. And yet if we're unaware of them, we're deprived of crucial information about our surroundings.

Perhaps worse than not being aware of our emotions is ignoring them. The worst thing we can do with our emotions is to ignore or stuff them down. But many of us have been taught that we should simply shake off any, especially negative, feelings we have and "get over it." The irony is that if we knew how to do this, wouldn't we have done it by now? We've also been taught that time heals all wounds. Who is this time guy anyway? If Mr. Time can heal us, why are so many couples carrying unhealed emotional hurts from years ago?

Emotions are incredibly valuable. Not in a way that suggests we should all indulge in emotional bliss, holding hands and singing "Kumbaya." Emotions are by definition irrational and illogical. But feelings are not right or wrong, good or bad. Instead, they are just a great source of information. God designed emotions to provide essential information regarding our needs, desires, and beliefs. Thus, they cannot be evaluated as right or wrong, good or bad. They're just information!

When we think about doing something that could hurt us, our emotions will tell us that this is not a good idea. Just by imagining what might happen, our emotions crank into action and give us the data to help us make better decisions.

Our emotions can inform and teach us if we let them. Have you ever had a gut feeling you can't explain, like when your child asks to spend the night over at someone's house you don't know or the snap judgment you make after meeting someone new? Now researchers are saying these feelings—or intuitions—are real and we should take our hunches seriously.[15] At least we should pursue the information our gut is trying to convey.

Not only do our emotions alert us through intuition, but they also let us know when our needs and desires are not being met. For example, when we feel lonely, that's our emotions telling us that our need for connection with other people is currently being unmet. When we feel afraid, our need for safety is unmet. When we feel rejected, it is our need for acceptance that is unmet.

Many people are not aware of what is going on inside of them emotionally, so they miss important information. For example, you might be hesitant to take action because of the fear of failing. You might be tentative about being open and vulnerable around people because you're afraid of being hurt. You might be resistant to sharing the desires of your heart out of the fear of being rejected.

Another source of important information is found in the difference between our primary and secondary emotions. A primary emotion is what we feel first. The secondary emotion is what it leads to.

Anger is a good example of a secondary emotion. There are many possible primary emotions that, when they are intense enough, can lead to anger. We might feel insulted, pressured, cheated, etc. If these feelings are at a low level, we are not likely to say we feel angry. But if they are intense, we commonly say we feel "angry." Depression is another example of a secondary emotion. Depression can include feeling discouraged, hopeless, lonely, isolated, misunderstood, overwhelmed, attacked, invalidated, unsupported, etc.

The problem with secondary emotions, such as anger and depression, is that they do not help us identify the real issue or our unmet emotional needs. When all I can say is "I feel angry," neither I nor anyone else knows what would help me feel better. But if I say I feel pressured or trapped or disrespected, it is much clearer what my need is and what would help me feel better.

In essence, emotions are a natural part of our God-given design and serve a good purpose to provide us with valuable information. When the heart is silenced, we are deprived of a rich resource for growth and relationship.

The most effective way of identifying our feelings is through emotional education. Simply put, you need to develop a "feelings" vocabulary.

Maybe that makes you think, "But isn't the key to understand *why* we are feeling the way we do?" No. It's actually more important to know *what* you're feeling than why you feel it. We need to experience and express a wide range of emotions, not just the pleasant ones. Otherwise, we have a limited awareness of who we are and are severely limited in our ability to learn important emotional lessons.

Contrary to popular culture, we do experience more than the "-*ad*" emotions: mad, bad, sad, and glad. Actually, there are more than three thousand words in the English language to describe emotions. Of these, one thousand or so are positive, and about two thousand are negative.[16] How many words do you have in your vocabulary to describe emotions? The more words you have, the more nuances of experience you can express and communicate.

If you're not sure how to identify your feelings, a good place to start is to simply ask yourself, "What am I feeling?" As you do this, remind yourself that you're after information. Don't judge your emotions, but instead see them as great sources of information. Then ask yourself, "What are my emotions trying to tell me?" What could it mean, for example, if you are feeling stressed out, worried, sad, fearful, hurt, or frustrated?

Once you identify your feelings don't try to figure out what to do with them. Don't try to fix how you feel. In this moment just work on learning how to become great at accurately identifying your feelings. You may want to ask yourself the following questions:

♡ Do I pay a lot of attention to how I feel?

♡ Do I notice my emotions as I experience them?

♡ What emotions do I frequently experience?

♡ What emotions are easy for me to express?

♡ What emotions are difficult for me to express?

♡ What emotions did I see expressed in my family growing up?

♡ What emotions were never expressed in my family growing up?

♡ Can I accurately name my feelings?

♡ Do I pay attention to my thoughts, beliefs, and actions that could be causing how I feel?

♡ Do I understand how my feelings influence my thoughts and actions?

♡ Am I aware of how my emotions impact my spouse?

It's so important to be able to identify your emotions. And thanks to Stacy, our therapist, you can no longer use just "fine" or "I'm okay."

I had a hard time coming up with precise feeling words, even though I have a doctorate in clinical psychology and deal with emotions all the time. My struggle was that I just couldn't put a name to what I was feeling. I just knew I was feeling something. I had never really developed this skill.

It is a skill, by the way. You can learn to accurately identify your feelings! To acquire this ability, you may want to use a "feelings list" that helped me convey more accurately how I felt. It's not a comprehensive list of emotions, but it is a start. Also, notice that the five major emotions vary in their intensity.

Frustration	Joy	Sadness	Hurt	Fear
bothered	content	sad	lonely	uncertain
annoyed	peaceful	depressed	homesick	worried
bitter	relaxed	distraught	abandoned	anxious
irritated	cheerful	despair	embarrassed	frightened
disgusted	satisfied	melancholy	shame	scared
exasperated	joyous	grief	guilt	nervous
angry	excited	helpless	foolish	afraid
furious	ecstatic	hopeless	humiliated	terrified
incensed	happy	miserable	hurt	overwhelmed

The best way to use this list is by accurately identifying your feelings on a daily basis. I made several copies of this list and kept one copy at the office and one at home in my Bible. I then reviewed the list several times throughout the day to notice how I was feeling. I also tried to do this before I went to bed at night.

This may sound bush-league or rudimentary, but I'm telling you that it worked. It didn't take me very long to develop a richer emotional vocabulary. The impact was not limited to the fact that I got better at expressing a wider range of emotions. It also helped me experience the flavor, intensity, and richness of emotions. It has definitely added spice to my life and marriage.

What I found was that this vocabulary exercise gave my heart a voice. Because I started allowing my feelings to matter, it helped me to validate those feelings. I quickly realized that although it's nice when Erin validates how I feel, I don't need her to do that.

Now, don't get me wrong. I certainly want her to validate me, but what happens when she's not at a place physically or emotionally to do that? Believe me, when I hurt her, I am the last person she wants to validate! If Erin is the only person to whom I turn for validation, I'm in big trouble.

Now *I* know how to do that job. Remember the old cliché "Wherever you go, there you are"? I should always be available to validate my own feelings. But in the past I was the last person to do that job so I was dependent on Erin. This wasn't fair to her, and it certainly wasn't honoring to me.

Remember, *God* is the creator of emotions—it was His design. Not only does God have deep feelings Himself, but He created us to experience emotions as well. Emotions exist to provide us with a valuable stream of information so that we can use this important information wisely.

What do we do with our emotions once we experience and identify them?

Management: Dealing with Your Emotions in Healthy Ways

If you tend to be more "heart" than "head," this section is for you.

As we've said, the best way to achieve a balance between the heart and the head is to learn to become aware of, recognize, and understand your emotions and then to constructively manage those emotions. Another way to say the same thing is this: feel what you want; manage what you do.

Once you discover the valuable stream of information found in your emotions, you'll get to use your mind and other resources to determine how to use that information wisely and how to express your emotions appropriately.

The key is managing your emotions. Notice the word *manage*. We like this idea much better than the thought of trying to *control* your feelings. When you control something, you try to rein it in or attempt to eliminate it. We don't want you to stifle or get rid of your feelings. This is what most of us have done with our feelings, which is exactly how we got into trouble in the first place. Instead, *feel what you want.*

You can't manage something you're not aware of or don't recognize and understand. I like how Dictionary.com defines the word *manage:* "Directing with a degree of skill or accomplishing something, sometimes despite difficulty or hardship." No one said that identifying and managing your feelings was easy. For me it has been like learning a foreign language. Author Haim Ginot has this to say about the importance of managing emotions:

> Emotions are part of our genetic heritage. Fish swim, birds fly, and people feel. Sometimes in our life we are sure to feel anger and fear, sadness and joy, greed and guilt, lust and scorn, delight and disgust. While we are not free to choose the emotions that arise in us, we are free to choose how and when to express them, provided we know what they are.[17]

When I say you should "manage what you do," I mean that you should use your brain and heart to guide your emotions toward success in relationships—to live wholeheartedly.

How do we learn to manage our emotions? This process begins by understanding what we typically do with our emotions.

Make Me Feel Better!

A woman's husband had been slipping in and out of a coma for several months, yet she had stayed by his bedside every single day. One day, he motioned for her to come nearer.

As she sat by him, he whispered to her, his eyes full of tears. "You know what? You have been with me all through the bad times. When I got fired, you were there to support me. When my business failed, you were there. When I got shot, you were by my side. When we lost the house, you stayed right here. When my health started failing, you were still by my side. . . . You know what?"

"What, dear?" she gently asked, smiling as her heart began to fill with warmth.

"When I think about it now, I think you bring me bad luck!"

This sensitive husband perfectly illustrates what most couples do with their emotions—they blame their spouses for how they feel. Once we see our spouses as the problem ("You make me so angry"), we usually see them as the solution as well ("If you just would stop being so critical, I wouldn't get so defensive"). If I see Erin as the problem, then I feel justified in my efforts to control, manipulate, or change her so that I can feel better.

We live in a culture of people who abdicate our emotions to others—to spouses, family, and friends. Our society wants others to make them feel better ("I'm going to verbalize how I feel so you can make me feel better"). Most men and women have not been taught how to manage their emotions in healthy ways.

Let's explore for a moment how we typically manage our feelings. Both men and women will do one or several of the following things with their emotions. They will:

- remain emotionally unaware or disconnect from their hearts
- judge, criticize, or disapprove of their emotions
- stuff, ignore, overlook, or disregard their feelings
- minimize, rationalize, or discount their emotions

♡ completely trust their feelings or believe they are true fact

♡ follow their emotions blindly, mindlessly act on them, or be impulsively lead by them

♡ recklessly spew or spray their feelings at others like an aerosol can

How do you typically handle your emotions? Are you oblivious? Do you ignore, judge, minimize, trust, blindly follow, or spray your emotions? The first step any time you are trying to grow is to gain the awareness that what you are doing is not working. Once you are clear on what you are presently doing to deal with your feelings, the next step in managing your emotions is to determine what you really want.

Identify What You Want

We all want something. When we are hurt, we want a solution, something that will make us feel better. Sometimes we might think that eating will make us feel better, that shopping will replace the hurt, that focusing on the children or other things will make us forget our troubles, or that drinking will dull the pain.

We spin lists of things that we believe might satisfy our wants. Or we reduce the conflict to that one, solitary thing that we think we need to feel satisfied: If only the other person would change so that I can feel better. If only I had a different boss, I would get the promotion at work. If she would just . . . or if my friends would only . . . then I could be happy.

Do you see the common thread in all this thinking? Two words: misplaced expectations.

When we expect people, places, or things to fulfill our wants, we end up disappointed. And anytime we put our expectations for help in the wrong place, the result is disappointment, frustration, hurt, and broken relationships. Many of us want the following things from our spouses and marriages:

- ♡ Acceptance—I want to be warmly received without condition.
- ♡ Grace—I want something good (i.e., forgiveness) that I don't deserve.
- ♡ Connection—I want to be united to others.
- ♡ Companionship—I want deep, intimate relationships.
- ♡ Success—I want to achieve or accomplish something.
- ♡ Self-determination—I want to have independence and free will.
- ♡ Understanding—I want to be known.
- ♡ Love—I want to feel attractive.
- ♡ Validation—I want to be valued for who I am.
- ♡ Competence—I want to have skills and abilities that bring success.
- ♡ Respect—I want to be admired and esteemed.
- ♡ Worth—I want to feel important.
- ♡ Honor—I want to feel like a priceless treasure.
- ♡ Commitment—I want to have unconditional security in relationships.
- ♡ Significance—I want to have meaning and purpose.
- ♡ Attention—I want to be noticed.
- ♡ Comfort—I want to feel a sense of well-being.
- ♡ Support—I want to be cared for.
- ♡ Approval—I want to be liked and accepted.

♡ Desire—I want to be sought after.

♡ Safety—I want to feel protected and secure.

♡ Affection—I want to feel fondness and warmth.

♡ Trust—I want to have faith in others.

♡ Hope—I want confidence that I will get what I love and desire.

♡ Joy—I want to feel satisfied and happy.

What do you do with the things you want? The key is to attend to your own feelings and wants—this is the opposite of controlling and manipulating others to get what you want. Attending to our own hearts begins by answering the following questions:

♡ Is there anything I need emotionally in this moment that I can provide myself?

♡ What would I want to hear or receive from my spouse or a friend in this moment that I can say to myself?

♡ What would taking care of my heart look like in this moment?

"Meet my own needs—are you for real?" you might be thinking. I know this might sound radically different from anything you've heard before. Remember, we live in a society that encourages codependency. But the truth is, God sent His Son so that we might have life and have it abundantly (see John 10:10). It doesn't say "I have given you your spouse so that you may have abundant life." Between you and the Lord, you can have an abundant life.

Christ has charged and equipped you to provide for your own needs. People are like God's assistants in our lives. When your spouse is not available, you can still do the job. If you want comfort, you can soothe yourself. If you want to feel valued, you can honor how God has uniquely gifted and blessed you with many strengths. When was the last time you made a list of your own gifts, talents, and character traits and then gave thanks to the Lord for how He's blessed you?

If you want validation, you can care about how you feel without judging or minimizing your feelings. If you want grace, you can forgive and have compassion for your poor choices. It's not an excuse or abdicating responsibility—it's just grace. If you want respect, you can respect yourself by taking great care of your body—the temple of the Holy Spirit.

Do you see what I mean by meeting your own needs? Now, the best is when your spouse joins in the process with you. That is the best of both worlds!

Go to the Lord

The secret weapon in managing your emotions is to ask the Lord to help care for your painful feelings and help meet your needs and wants. The cool part is that God is always available, and His desire is to restore the brokenhearted: "He heals the brokenhearted and binds up their wounds" (Psalm 147:3). The key is to ask God from your heart and not with your brain: "The LORD hears them; he delivers them from all their troubles" (Psalm 34:17).

Lord . . .

- ♡ Are there any other feelings that I'm not aware of?
- ♡ Is there anything that I'm not seeing that You know I need?
- ♡ What is Your perspective on this issue?

♡ What is the truth about me and the situation I'm in?

♡ Is there anything that I need to take responsibility for?

♡ What do I need to seek forgiveness for?

♡ Who is the person that You want me to be in this moment—the person You created me to be?

Do you know the real reason you should take your emotions to the Lord? Sure it's wonderful to have Christ care for you, but the primary purpose is to get your heart back open. The real danger when you get hurt or frustrated is that your heart shuts down. And when you have a closed heart, look out. People make some of the worst choices and decisions when they have closed hearts (e.g., affairs, drugs, alcohol, deception, etc.). You need both your heart and your brain to make Christlike decisions.

How Are You Contributing to Your Feelings?

Another way to manage your emotions is to clarify how *you* may have contributed to how you feel.

I can hear the objections: "Hey, I didn't do anything; she's the one who criticized me!" Or, "I asked him to do one simple thing, and he forgot!" But one of the most important lessons I've learned over the years is that it is never 100 percent the other person's fault when you experience hurtful emotions.

It's good to ask yourself: *"What am I doing to cause my emotions to be stirred up?"* Look at your own thoughts, interpretations, judgments, perceptions, expectations, thought patterns, fears, past hurts, beliefs, family-of-origin issues, and so on. We all do more than we think to intensify our own feelings.

Take me, for example. I remember one time when Erin and I were going out for dinner. We'd had several arguments throughout the week, and we weren't in the best of places relationally. We really needed a nice evening out.

As I pulled up from work, Erin met me in the driveway. As she climbed into the car, I could tell that she was upset about something. *Great*, I thought. *What did I do now?* I ran through a mental checklist of the day to see if I could remember having done something wrong. *Nothing*, I determined. *I didn't do anything!*

I continued to stir, watching Erin sit, silent—obviously mad at me.

I finally reached a boiling point. "Why do you always do this when we're going out on a date?" I shouted, "Why are you so mad at me? What did I do?"

Ready to defend myself at whatever she had to say, I was taken aback by her response.

"What on earth is going on with you?" Erin asked, bewildered. "I'm not mad at you. I just had a difficult phone call with a friend who said some very hurtful things to me. I was just about to ask you for some advice on what you think I should do."

"Oh" was all I could muster at that moment. Talk about feeling like a complete idiot.

The point is that *I* was the one who had exacerbated my own feelings. I was the one who had made the faulty interpretation of Erin's mood and silence. I was the one who had contributed to my emotions getting all stirred up. And then of course I now really had done something wrong by accusing her.

What does this look like in your life? Reflect upon these questions:

♡ Do you jump to conclusions or make snap judgments?

♡ Do you have a habit of miscommunication and misinterpretation?

♡ Do you have negative beliefs about your spouse that may have contributed to your feelings?

♡ Do you interpret your spouse's behavior without checking it out first?

♡ Do you give your loved ones the benefit of the doubt?

♡ What were you expecting would or wouldn't happen?

♡ Do you have any faulty thought patterns?

♡ What past hurts or issues might be contributing to this situation?

♡ What issues from your family of origin or experiences you had growing up might be factors in how you feel?

By asking you to look at how you might be contributing to your own feelings, I'm not saying that your feelings are your fault. This isn't meant to absolve others of their poor choices. But you can't change people. We are responsible for our feelings. You can only change your own beliefs, thoughts, and behaviors. Let the Lord deal with the other person.

Obviously, a part of managing your emotions in a healthy way is being willing to keep short accounts and lovingly confront others. But this should happen only after you've dealt with *you* first—after you've managed your own emotions and have gotten your heart back open.

CHOOSE A HEALTHY RESPONSE TO YOUR EMOTIONS

Once you have recognized and understood your emotions, have gone to the Lord in prayer, and identified what you want and how you might have contributed to your feelings, now is when you decide what course of action is best.

Remember, feel what you want; manage what you do. With all the pertinent information acquired, what would be the best action to take? In order to answer this question, think about:

♡ What hasn't worked in the past?
♡ What has worked before?
♡ What are my options and choices?
♡ What would a healthy response look like?

In the past when dealing with your emotions, perhaps you ignored or stuffed your feelings, judged, minimized, saw them as fact, impulsively acted upon them, or spewed your emotions on others—things that never ultimately work. These choices may provide temporary relief, but in the end we feel dead inside, hard-hearted, out of control, and guilty, and our personal integrity takes a major hit.

The key is to think about what has worked in the past or might work now to manage your emotions in a healthy way. For example, you can do things like:

♡ Take a few deep breaths.
♡ Go to the Lord in prayer.
♡ Stand up and stretch.
♡ Read the Bible.

♡ Review the feelings list to identify additional significant feelings.

♡ Listen to praise and worship music.

♡ Lower your voice and speak softly.

♡ Go for a walk or jog.

♡ Take a "time out," but let the other person know that you'll work out the issue later.

♡ Journal your feelings.

♡ Talk to your spouse.

♡ Call a friend.

♡ Clean something.

♡ Exercise.

♡ Watch TV.

♡ Do laundry.

♡ Seek first to understand rather than being understood.

♡ Wash the car.

♡ Play with the kids.

♡ Mow the lawn.

♡ Listen to your iPod.

♡ Read a book.

♡ Go for a drive.

You see, there are plenty of healthy choices you can make to better manage your emotions. What is missing from the list that you've done before that worked? Be sure to ask several other people you respect what they do to help them manage or regulate their emotions. At every conference I always ask the audience for their ideas. I have learned so much over the years and now use many of their ideas in my own life (except mowing the lawn—I hate to mow!).

The key is to do the things on the above list without ruminating on what made you so upset or hurt in the first place. I call this *perseverating*.

Perseverating is when you go over something obsessively or redundantly. One marriage expert calls this "distress-maintaining thoughts." We must replace these distress-maintaining thoughts with soothing and validating thoughts like *We'll get through this* or *I'm sure she's just having a rough day* or *I know he really loves me even though I don't feel it right now*.

The more options and choices you have, the more likely you'll be to choose a healthy response the next time you find yourself in an emotionally intense situation.

Although I don't want to debate any of the above ideas directly, here is a quick way to assess if what you do is actually helpful or not: if what you are doing is ultimately a healthy choice, then everyone should benefit from it. My wife has often challenged me that watching TV isn't a healthy way to manage my feelings. But if watching TV helps me cool down or zone out for a moment, and if this leads me to identify my feelings and respond appropriately to my emotions, then I would argue that everyone involved benefited from my choice. If this helps get me to a better place emotionally, then my wife and children benefit, I benefit, and the Lord is honored. The only one who doesn't win is the Evil One. Remember:

Do not conform any longer to the pattern of this world, but be transformed by the renewing of your mind. Then you will be able to test and approve what God's will is— his good, pleasing and perfect will. (Romans 12:2)

We trust you see how important your heart is and that your feelings matter. Learning to identify and manage your emotions in healthy ways is the key to unleashing the voice of your heart.

In the next three chapters we will show you three forces at work to disconnect you from your heart (wounds, fears, and exhaustion) and how you can counteract these deadly forces and keep your heart open.

Let's begin with the wounded heart.

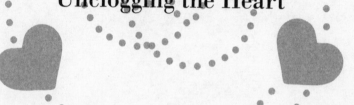

PART TWO
Unclogging the Heart

Chapter 3
The Wounded Heart

As he thinks in his heart, so is he.

—Proverbs 23:7 NKJV

Search me, O God, and know my heart; test me and know my anxious thoughts.

—Psalm 139:23

THIRTY-SIX DEGREES outside. No ice on the driveway, but there might as well be. The panhandle of Texas gets pretty cold in December. Thirteen-year-old Christina shoots free throws. Her dad, Bill, retrieves the balls and offers advice . . . "elbow in, follow through high, eyes looking just over the front of the rim, use your legs, believe in yourself."

Three hours earlier Christina had the same-length shot, a free throw, to win the game for her team. With her dad's voice echoing in her head, *"Games are won and lost at the free-throw line,"* she took a deep breath, went through her routine. She shot and missed. Despite Christina's twenty points, her team lost.

So now Christina practices. Bill is encouraging and supportive. He really loves her, believes in her, and wants to see her reach her full potential. He was an amazing football and baseball player in college. He would have played in the pros if not for the poor timing of the military draft board. Bill married and had two daughters. Christina is the younger of the two and the more passionate about sports. She loves her dad, admires him, and wants to please him. So now Christina practices despite being cold and tired.

On the surface, there is nothing significant about this interaction. But the heart is not on the surface. On a deeper level, something significant is happening to Christina. The Enemy is subtly using her interactions with her dad to convince her of the lie that she will never be able to play well enough.

On her heart, the Enemy etches the words YOU ARE NOT GOOD ENOUGH. When she is mistreated by boyfriends, the lie on her heart is confirmed: YOU ARE NOT GOOD ENOUGH. When she makes the all-state basketball team and her dad challenges her to try to be an all-American in college, the message on her heart is again confirmed: YOU ARE NOT GOOD ENOUGH. Christina's heart is wounded.

She is not alone. We all have wounds. Different authors or psychologists might call them hurts, lies, fears, arrows, messages . . . but they are all the same. Life events create wounds— painful hurts, lies, and messages that try to define who we are. When these wounds occur on a heart level, the result is profound. The wounds impact the way we live our lives and influence how we interact with people, especially our spouses.

Understanding your heart and its role in life is essential to living to the fullest. Hopefully, you are beginning to see that your heart does matter, that your feelings are significant, and that your ability to love is dependent on keeping an open heart.

In these next three chapters, you will begin to identify what forces have worked to disconnect you from your heart and how you can counteract these forces. Diagnosing where you have lost heart and getting your heart back in the game are the keys to a wholehearted marriage.

THE ASSAULT ON THE HEART

We desire to live life wholeheartedly: open and connected. God designed us to live this way, but the Enemy wants the opposite. So our hearts, the vital center of who we are, are attacked. I think John Eldredge, in his book *Waking the Dead*, summed it up the best:

> I find it almost hard to believe a case must be made that the heart is . . . well, at the heart of it all. Of life. Of each person. Of God. And of Christianity.
>
> It is diabolical, despicable, and is downright evil. This bears the mark of the enemy. The enemy knows how vital the heart is, even if we do not, and all his forces are fixed upon its destruction. For if he can disable or deaden your heart, then he has effectively foiled the plan of God, which was to create a world where love reigns.
>
> By taking out your heart, the enemy takes out you, and you are essential to the Story. Once you begin to see with the eyes of your heart, once you have begun to know it is true from the bottom of your heart, it will change everything. The story of your life is the story of the long and brutal assault on your heart by the one who knows what you and your marriage could be and fears it.[1]

The story of our lives is the story of the long, brutal assault on our hearts. The Enemy cunningly uses our life circumstances and significant interactions to wound our hearts.

Christina's wounds were subtle. Growing up in a loving Christian home, the Enemy had to work really hard to twist her dad's demanding encouragement into a deeply negative message about herself. Sometimes the wounds are subtle, and other times they are pretty easy to identify. Over the years, we have heard hundreds of life stories and the subsequent wounds produced:

- ♡ As a high school wrestler, Mark won the state championship as a junior. His senior year during a particularly long match, he allowed his opponent to pin him to get the competition over with. The Enemy used that circumstance to begin etching QUITTER on Mark's heart.

- ♡ Elizabeth was the youngest of five children. Her parents were loving and attentive but also thankful when their last child was finally off to college. Elizabeth's heart was broken the first time she came home from college and her parents did not even get out of the chair to greet her. She began feeling unimportant.

- ♡ Jenny's parents often left her to stay at her cousin's house despite her pleading to the contrary. Many of those nights, her uncle would come into the room where she slept and climb into bed with her. She would cry for help and beg him to stop, but he didn't. She clearly got the message: *what you want does not matter.* And, even more important: *you don't matter.*

♡ Will's dad walked out of the house when Will was eight. He never returned, never wrote a card, never called, never sent a gift on Will's birthday. He was gone. Will got the message: *you are unwanted.*

♡ Andy was an amazingly talented artist, but art was not valued by his friends or the coaches at school. On the day of the Presidential Physical Fitness Test, Andy was not able to do a single pull-up or sit-up. Everyone laughed at him. Andy began feeling like a failure.

♡ Sandy's mom was always conscious of Sandy's appearance. She was quick to point out when Sandy gained a few pounds, always ready to tell her she would never find a good man if she got fat. The Enemy deeply etched this lie onto Sandy's heart: *your value is based on your appearance.*

♡ The divorce was sudden. Bobby did not even know his parents were having trouble. It did not make sense to his six-year-old heart that his parents were living in separate houses. Maybe if he had been a better kid, then he could have kept them together. Instead, he clearly understood: *you have no control.*

♡ From as early as Jack could remember, his dad drank. The people in town made fun of his dad. Jack would plead with his father to quit, but the drinking never stopped. Jack heard loud and clear: *you're not worth it.*

♡ Chris wanted to serve the Lord. He finally got a chance as a youth minister in a small town. But his innovative ways were not appreciated, and soon some of the parents began spreading rumors about him and making up lies. Chris left the ministry, intent on never returning, tired of the rejection.

♡ Connie's dad was the life of the party, fun and engaging. On the other hand, he could be volatile and angry. Connie never learned how to predict which mood her dad would be in. The Enemy began telling her heart: *you are powerless.*

♡ Parker was different, and all the kids at school knew it. No one sat with him at lunch, no one played with him, no one even talked to him. He left middle school with a clear message that he would always be alone.

As you can see, the Enemy can use any circumstance and any person to deeply wound our hearts.

Let's review the process:

1. The Enemy uses life circumstances to create wounds.

2. The wounds come with messages that tell us something about ourselves (e.g., you are not valuable).

3. The messages are almost always unconscious—they are etched on our hearts without our awareness.

4. The messages are lies—they are not true about us (e.g., you really are valuable, but the lie tells you otherwise).

5. The messages on our hearts affect how we see ourselves and how we interact with the world.

Why does the Enemy attack our hearts? Because, remember, the heart is the vital center of who we are. Whatever is going on in the heart affects every other aspect of our lives. As a man thinks in his heart, so is he (see Proverbs 23:7 NKJV). Thus the battle is over control of our hearts.

God wants our hearts filled with the truth of who He created us to be. From this full authentic place, our hearts will be open and loving. However, the Enemy wants our hearts filled with lies and false messages. He uses the wounds to convince us to close down and shut off from others. Marriages cannot succeed when hearts are shut down.

The lies, wounds, and messages written on our hearts have far-reaching ramifications. Let's look back at the people listed above and see how the initial messages impacted their lives and relationships.

♡ Mark (I'm a quitter), the high school wrestler, came to marriage counseling because his wife says he never follows through on commitments and he is always quitting when the going gets tough.

♡ Elizabeth (I'm not important) constantly questions her husband, whom she believes focuses more attention on work than on her.

♡ Jenny (I don't matter) sought value and worth in a string of sexual relationships with men.

♡ Will (I am not wanted) works constantly to please people and tells them what they want to hear so they will want to be with him. His behavior is so extreme that his wife says she does not even know who he really is.

♡ Andy (I'm a failure) works sixteen-hour days in the business world. He hates his job but is determined to prove he can be successful.

♡ Sandy (My value is based on my appearance) has

suffered from a string of eating disorders. She is passing on her unrealistic expectations about body image to her kids.

♡ Bobby (I have no control) is overbearing and dominating in his marriage. His wife can't even go to the grocery store without first checking with her controlling husband.

♡ Jack (I'm not worth it) has let his wife and two business partners run all over him. They have taken his self-esteem and his money. He suffers from depression and once attempted suicide.

♡ Chris (I'm always rejected) is very meek and quiet. He refuses to speak up in a crowd or take risks in his life. He searches for people's acceptance in every interaction.

♡ Connie (I am powerless) married a fun, successful man. He gets angry and violent just like her dad. She is so used to the cycle that she just takes whatever he dishes out, never saying a word to anyone outside the home.

♡ Parker (I'm alone) clings to his wife and will do anything she asks. Their marriage is very codependent because he cannot afford to lose her.

These are the stories of our lives. Things happen to us in this fallen world we live in. People hurt us. These early incidents and interactions lead to wounds on our vulnerable hearts. The wounds turn into false messages about who we really are. We continue in life with these messages pushing us to behave in ways that are unhealthy. The messages are so powerful that we eventually shut down our hearts to protect ourselves. With our hearts disengaged, our marriages suffer or end.

Remember Christina from the start of the chapter? She became wounded by her dad's pressure to excel in basketball. The wound turned into the message that she was not good enough. That internal message etched on her heart actually pushed her to do better. She became an all-state basketball player. Unfortunately, no amount of earthly success could remove the message from her heart. She still felt not good enough.

Christina is the girl I (Shawn) met in the bar in Denton, Texas, who eventually married me. We both attended the University of North Texas. She was a scholarship athlete still trying to prove she was good enough but also rebelling against her parents in a mild show of independence. I was a graduate student in psychology, trying to figure myself out.

Over four years of dating, we fought and broke up almost as much as we were happy together. Christina's fear of not being good enough extended beyond the basketball court and into every area of her life. If she had a bad game, the "not good enough" button was triggered. If I wanted to go be with my friends one night, the "not good enough" button was triggered. If she did poorly on an exam, the "not good enough" button was triggered. If she fought with her roommates, the "not good enough" button was triggered. Christina lost all her self-esteem and almost sank into depression. The wound on her heart from earlier in life was simply that powerful.

It didn't help that I had my own wounds that were messing up our relationship. After losing my mom, I shut my heart down and withdrew from people. My wounded heart got a few key messages etched on it—you are not acceptable, and you are helpless. These messages made me a fearful, lonely person.

I didn't feel like Christina would ever accept me for who I was, so I worked really hard to impress her. I also hated feeling helpless, so I would become overcontrolling and manipulative in my attempts to get her to love me. Christina was pretty strong willed and very resistant to being controlled and manipulated. Needless to say, we had a volatile relationship. Our friends loved to double date with us because we were very entertaining. At any moment, we could have a major blowup for all to witness.

Thankfully, Christina and I finally got the help we needed. Some loving, insightful counselors taught us to stop fighting each other. They helped us to see that our problems came from a deeper place. The early wounds on our hearts had created some messages that were now sabotaging our relationship. Instead of trying to change each other, Christina and I had to first focus on ourselves.

Christina and I are not unique. I have seen hundreds of couples derailed in their marriages because of the effect of early wounds. The wounded heart prevents us from living wholeheartedly. The wounds give entry to messages and lies that prevent us from understanding the truth of who we really are. We close down our hearts to protect ourselves from more wounds. Thus we miss out on authentic marriages where love can flow freely between us and our spouses.

We must deal with the wounds. And we must replace the lies with the truth. Only then will we be free to open our hearts.

UNCLOGGING THE WOUNDED HEART

We long for a great marriage. Amazing marriages happen when two people are wholeheartedly engaged inside their covenant relationship. Being fully open allows love (along with peace, patience, kindness, goodness . . .) to flow freely between spouses.

As we have seen, the Enemy wants to prevent this. Life circumstances and significant people have a way of wounding us.

Our job is to heal these wounds so we can get back to whole-hearted engagement.

Moving from a wounded heart to a healthy heart is a three-step process: you must identify the wounds and false messages, you must replace the messages with the truth, and you must nurture and care for your heart. Let's look at each one of these.

Step 1: Identify the Wounds and Messages

We must identify the wounds and messages that have attacked our hearts. None of us escapes this world unharmed. None of us is immune to the power of the Enemy to inscribe our hearts with lies and negative messages.

Before we even start the healing process, we need to counter a few arguments you may have about this process.

1. "I'm not wounded, because I had a perfect family and a perfect childhood." As hard as it is to believe that "perfect" exists in this fallen world, we know there's a chance that you may have been raised in a great home. But even then, you were exposed to dating relationships, peer interactions, school systems, and more, all of which could have been used to create wounds. No matter how great your childhood was, no one escapes those years without wounds.

2. "I don't like to blame everything on my past." Good for you! We don't either. In this exercise we are not blaming our pasts. The goal is not to make someone else responsible for what has happened to us in life. However, we must take the time to

understand our pasts and the influence the past has on our current situation.

3. "I don't believe all this stuff about *the Enemy*." No problem. Call it what you want: life, our world, the culture, circumstances. We believe the Enemy is underlying all of this—but even if you don't, the principles still hold true. It does not really matter whom you attribute the wounds to. It is only important that you identify the messages and lies accurately.

Near the very start of the Bible, Adam and Eve ate of the forbidden fruit. They responded to the sudden guilt they felt by covering themselves, hiding, and blaming. When God asked why they were behaving so strangely, Adam replied, "I was afraid" (Genesis 3:10). With the eating of the fruit and the fall of Adam and Eve, the Enemy successfully introduced fear into our world.

Like the first couple on earth, we all experience fears, lies, and false messages. Below is a list of the most common messages we find on people's hearts after we talk with them in a counseling setting. They say they feel one or more of the following emotions:

- ♡ Rejected
- ♡ Abandoned
- ♡ Disconnected
- ♡ Failure
- ♡ Helpless
- ♡ Powerless
- ♡ Inadequate
- ♡ Inferior
- ♡ Invalidated

- ♡ Unloved
- ♡ Undesirable
- ♡ Not good enough
- ♡ Worthless
- ♡ Devalued
- ♡ Unaccepted
- ♡ Judged
- ♡ Ignored
- ♡ Unimportant
- ♡ Misunderstood
- ♡ Wrongly portrayed
- ♡ Disrespected
- ♡ Unwanted
- ♡ Defective

Your job is to identify which of these messages is etched on your heart. There may be more than one. That's okay. You may be feeling something that is not on this list, and that's okay too. The important thing is to identify the messages.

There are three paths to follow that will reveal what is on your heart. You can try one or all three.

First, don't try to do it alone. God wants to help. In Psalm 139:23 David said, "Search me, O God, and know my heart; test me and know my anxious thoughts." David was asking God to search his heart and let him know what fears and messages were written there.

You can do the same thing. Ask God to search your heart for fears, lies, and harmful messages. What does He see?

I know God wants to give you the answer. He hates those lies and messages falsely inscribed on your heart. I will never forget the night he helped me with a real dangerous message that was forming in the heart of our daughter, Taylor.

To set the scene, you would have to understand the nightly routine at our house. It seems a little chaotic most nights—herding kids to the bath, forcing them to brush teeth, getting last-minute drinks of water, and finally drifting toward bed. Taylor is pretty compliant. We would send her to bed, poke our heads in, tell her we were proud of her and that we loved her, and maybe say a quick prayer.

Then we'd have to move on because our son, Cade, needed a lot more intervention to get him into bed. Cade is very active, and to get him to sleep requires sitting in bed with him to hold him still. After ten minutes or so of keeping him in bed, his little body finally gives up the fight, and he falls fast asleep, exhausted from running wholeheartedly all day.

One night I was lying there praying while I held Cade in his bed. As I asked God to protect, nurture, and grow my kids, I began to sense God was telling me something. I listened closely as God revealed to me what was going on in Taylor's heart across the hall. God told me that Enemy was beginning to etch the message *You are not important* on Taylor's heart, because we spent so much more time with her brother at night than we did with her.

Obviously, our intention was not to communicate this to her. But our intentions did not really matter. I told Christina what was going on, and we immediately equalized the amount of time we spent with each child at night. A few weeks later while lying in bed with Taylor, she told me that spending those minutes together at night was one of her favorite times of the day and that it really made her feel special. Thank God for revealing that lie in time for us to correct the situation.

It is really cool that God will reveal what is going on in the hearts of our children, and our spouses for that matter. But don't start there. Begin by asking God what is written on *your* heart. As we have shown you, He cares what is going on in there. Your heart is the place where He wants to meet with you. It is the place where He wants to pour His love. It is all He sees when He looks at you. So you can bet He knows what the walls look like in that heart of yours. Be like King David, the man after God's own heart, and ask Him.

The second way to find out what is written on your heart is to think back over any significant moments you can recall from your childhood (traumatic events, disappointments, times you were hurt). What were you feeling? What did you say to yourself, or what message did you receive from the incident?

From the examples of people with wounded hearts at the start of the chapter, you can see that traumatic events can take many forms. Some are more obvious, like your parents' divorce, sexual molestation, death of a significant person in your life, extreme neglect, abuse, etc. Watch almost any person they highlight on the Biography Channel, and you will easily identify the traumatic events that influenced their lives.

Other events are more subtle but no less powerful, such as frequent relocations, poor peer interactions, not meeting expectations in grades or performances, etc. One of my pastors talks about a significant moment in his life being the time he did not make the twelve-year-old baseball all-star team when all of his friends did.

My mom's death was a very traumatic event in my life. As I explored that event further in counseling, I learned that other incidents afterward also profoundly impacted my heart.

For example, once we were approaching the start of a new school year, so we told our dad that we needed new school clothes. This had always been mom's job, so none of us really knew what getting these clothes entailed. Remember, my dad was a cowboy and a very practical man. Since he was headed to the feed store, he took us along. In those days in Texas, you could get clothes right in the back of the feed store.

Well, you can imagine what those clothes looked like. Cowboy-boot-cut Wrangler jeans in multiple colors, shirts with snaps for buttons and checkered patterns, and corduroy sport coats with patches on the sleeves. Dad outfitted us with new school clothes right there in the feed store.

That probably would have been fine except for the fact that we went to school in a neighborhood in Houston, Texas. The kids in our school were either preppy upper middle class or urban hip-hop. I was the only one dressed up like Roy Rogers. And you'd better believe the other kids noticed. I was consistently picked on because of my wardrobe, I did not have many friends, and I felt very alone. On a deeper level, my heart was being wounded . . . inscribed with the word REJECTION.

In your own search, first consider what events may have opened the door to heart wounds (e.g., made fun of at school). Then identify what you were feeling (hurt and alone). Third, what did you unconsciously say to yourself based on the incident and what you were feeling (I am not acceptable)?

Our hearts are amazingly valuable and incredibly vulnerable. Just identifying the traumatic events is not enough. You have to dig deeper to see how the events impacted your heart. Two people can experience the same event and be impacted in very different ways on a heart level.

I know two good men who both made the same horrible mistake earlier in life. They both engaged in premarital sex with women they were seriously dating. Both women got pregnant. In both instances, the couples decided to go through with an abortion to terminate the pregnancies.

Twenty years later, both of these men regret their decisions and still feel guilt. For one man, the message he received from this traumatic event was *You are unworthy to do any kind of ministry.* For the other man, he clearly still hears to this day that he is a *failure* because he made the wrong choice in the biggest decision of his life. Same traumatic event, different messages. Both damaging.

What were those events or interactions in your life, and what messages did you take away from them?

Third, think back to a recent conflict with your spouse. What were you feeling? Review the word list above—did you feel any of those things?

Our spouses have a way of triggering these wounds deep inside us. It makes sense: we grant to our spouses access to the most vulnerable part of who we are. With all that access, our spouses have the greatest ability to do us harm. Our spouses' words or actions can easily tap into the messages and lies that we bring into our marriages.

Christina brought her wounds into our marriage, and I brought mine. I cannot tell you how many times I have triggered the harmful messages inside her. Sometimes it is obvious, like when I say, "You are incapable of sticking to a budget." She naturally hears, *I am not good enough.* Sometimes it's more subtle and very unintentional, such as when I say, "Cade seems to be falling behind his peers a little in his reading." Christina hears, *I'm not good enough as a mom and teacher to our son.*

The wounds and messages come with us whether we want them to or not. Once, I came home from work and said, "You guys must have had a great time playing today." Christina assumed I saw the house was not cleaned up and that I was making a sarcastic remark about her housecleaning. (I have thought that before, but this time I swear my motives were pure.) All she heard was, *I am not a good enough wife.*

I'm the same way. Many times Christina has tapped into my old messages about being not acceptable. When our finances, our kids, or our lives get out of control, I frequently feel helpless, just like I did when my mom died. I know there is no comparison between those events but the lie gets triggered in my wounded heart just the same. My interactions with Christina have given me the ability to identify what those messages are.

So think back to a conflict that you have had recently with your spouse or some other significant loved one (your parents and your kids can trigger these messages pretty well). I know, you felt angry, mad, frustrated, or upset. Dig a little deeper. . . . Did you also feel hurt or scared? Good, now keep going deeper. What did the conflict make you say about yourself? Look back at the list above and identify one or two messages that fit.

Great work. You have hopefully begun to identify the lies and hurtful messages that have wounded your heart. Now let's get to work cleaning those messages off so that they can no longer drive you to act and feel in ways you don't want to. Clearing off those messages also gives you the freedom to begin to open your heart again.

Step 2: Replace the Messages with the Truth

The first step was to identify the hurtful messages going around in your heart. The next is to replace those messages with truth.

The Enemy is the author of lies. Anything he writes on your heart, any message he creates, will not be true. Now that you have identified the lies, messages, and fears, isn't it great to know that they are complete fabrications? Once you know what's being falsely said about you, it's time to replace those things with the truth. It is not a difficult process, but it is something that you are going to need a little help with.

You may be saying, "I see the message on my heart now, and I already know that it is not true." Unfortunately, it is not that simple. You see, the message is etched on your *heart*. Your knowledge that it is false is in your *head*. In a battle between your head and heart, your heart will win every time. You cannot outsmart or outrationalize what is written on your heart. Your heart is more powerful than your head. Remember, the Bible tells us as a man thinks in his *heart* so he is, not as a man thinks in his head.

Just as there were three ways to identify your hurtful messages, there are three places to turn to in order to find out the truth about you and your heart.

First, look to God, who is the ultimate Source of truth. When we approach God in prayer, we get to speak to Jesus and the Holy Spirit. That is good news because they know a thing or two about what is true and what is a lie.

Jesus referred to Himself as "the way and *the truth* and the life" (John 14:6). When Jesus was telling His friends about His departure, He comforted them with the news that He would soon be sending a helper: "I will ask the Father, and he will give you another Counselor to be with you forever—the Spirit of Truth" (John 14:16–17). Isn't it great to know that the role of the Holy Spirit is to remind us of the truth of who we were created to be? All you have to do is ask.

In the intensive model of marital counseling that we teach, couples come to us with all kinds of wounds and false messages. The most healing part of the entire process occurs when the individuals take their wounds before the Lord and ask Him what is true. Many of the people who come have never heard God speak to them and are very skeptical that He will. Despite their doubts, time after time God reveals the truth about them when they ask.

One man really stands out in my memory. The message on his heart was that he was worthless, so he diligently sought the Lord for the truth. After two days, he still had heard nothing, and he was growing fearful. On the third morning, he came to breakfast with a beaming smile and a clean heart. That morning in the shower, God had told him that he was not worthless, but that he was amazingly valuable.

In the session later that day, a disagreement with his wife caused him to feel worthless again. He went to his room at the break and returned with a wet head. He said he had gotten back in the shower, and God had again reminded him that he was amazingly valuable. Before long, the entire group wanted to take turns in that shower so they could hear from the Lord.

You don't need a shower to hear from God. He wants to answer you. The Holy Spirit wants to remind you of the truth. Take your wounds, fears, lies, and harmful messages to Him. Jesus said that He came to heal the brokenhearted. Let Him heal your wounded heart by speaking the truth into you. Am I really helpless and unacceptable? Is Christina really not good enough? Are you really a failure, alone, unlovable, inadequate? Whatever the message, take it to God. Wait and listen for an answer.

The lyrics of the Casting Crowns song "Voice of Truth" capture the essence of this point. The song talks about a voice that tells the singer he's a complete failure. But there's another voice, God's voice of truth, telling another story altogether. God's voice tells him that he doesn't have to fear, because this will all work out to God's glory. In the song, the singer chooses to listen to the voice of truth.

That's what you must do too. The Enemy uses people and events in your past to lie to you. But the Lord, the voice of truth, longs to speak life into your wounded heart.

Not only is the Lord going to speak truth into the lies you've bought into from your past, but He will also help you apply His truth to what people say to you in the present.

Looking back, the most helpful thing I (Greg) have learned is to listen to what people say and then take those things to the Lord and pursue His truth. In the past, when someone would criticize, judge, evaluate, critique, scrutinize, or share an opinion with me, I would take it as fact and treat it as a certainty. More damaging was that I allowed their words to become truth in my life.

The reality is that people are human. As human beings, we are flawed and have a sin nature. Simply because we feel or believe something doesn't make it true. People have their own expectations, family-of-origin issues, past experiences, beliefs, values, and so on that *always* color their perception of the truth.

Anytime someone shares something, it is only "true" from that person's point of view, and he or she will have his or her own "stuff" intertwined with the truth. Think of it as a big twisted ball of fishing line. To untangle the truth from their stuff, I take to the Lord what they say. I no longer allow people to be the source of truth in my life.

When Erin shares her feelings or frustrations about me, I listen (to the best of my ability!) and then tell her that I will check out what she's saying with the Lord. I remember the first time I ever said this to her. She looked at me (you know the look) and said, "This is just another clever ploy to get out of hearing me!" Although this was far from the truth, I knew that I probably deserved her skepticism.

Instead of arguing with her, I went to the Lord in prayer. Later on that day I felt a real peace in my heart about what she had shared. But because it had been the Lord who had brought me to a place of conviction, I was instantly able to take responsibility for my choices. It's not our mates' job to convince us. That's God's role.

Even when someone comes to me and says, "The Lord told me to say this . . ." or "God revealed this to me . . . ," I am cautious.

God certainly uses people to speak His truth into my life. But I am convinced that when we hear things from people (even apparent words from the Lord), we should always check it out by going to the Source of truth.

And what is the Source of truth? John 16:13 makes it pretty clear that it's the Holy Spirit: "When he, the Spirit of truth, comes, he will guide you into all truth." The Lord will always guide us to His truth if we ask.

So now, no matter what someone says, I check it out with Him. Literally while the person is still talking to me, I am praying, *Lord, you hear what he is saying about me—is this truth? What are You trying to teach me?* I have been doing this for several years now, and I consistently have experienced the Lord's revealing His truth when I ask. The key is that you must seek Him with an open heart and mind. He is always faithful.

Second, look for the truth in the Bible. While the voice of the Lord is probably the most powerful way to learn the truth, God knew that we would need even more help. So He wrote a bunch of stuff down in the Bible. The Bible is filled with scriptures that tells us the truth about who we were created to be.

Nathan is a friend of mine who has done an outstanding job of lining up the truth of Scripture against the wounds in his heart. At about eight years of age, Nathan was introduced to pornography through a *Playboy* magazine. He can even tell you the place in their attic where he and his brother hid the magazine.

Over the years, the Enemy used pornography to capture and wound Nathan's heart. Nathan came to believe that he was a phony and a failure. His wounded heart came with him into his marriage, and the lies prevented him from being the husband he wanted to be. Nathan had to do something.

He turned to the Bible and began finding verses that spoke against the messages inscribed on his heart. He landed on two passages in particular: "I am the righteousness of God" (from 2 Corinthians 5:21) and "I am ever captivated by my wife's [Jane's] love" (from Proverbs 5:19). He committed to memorize these verses and a few others, reciting them several times a day.

At first he did not even believe it was true, so he recited the verses quietly when he thought others might be within earshot. But as time passed, he got a little bolder. One day, he was saying the verses out loud in his living room, when his wife came around the corner. He felt embarrassed, but she looked at him lovingly and confirmed that she could see the fruit of his changing heart. Nathan used the truth of Scripture to heal the wound and erase the messages on his heart.

Nathan had read his Bible for years (his dad was a pastor), but he did not tap into the healing power of Scripture until he got specific with what he was looking for. God's general promises are great, but the key is to get very specific with the verses you choose. Find verses that line up right against your lies and false messages.

The Enemy has leveled a specific attack against you, with specific lies and messages. Those wounds must be healed by using specific truth to counterattack. For example, if your fear is being alone or abandoned, you might want to memorize and continuously recite, "I will never leave you nor forsake you" (Joshua 1:5).

The Bible is an incredibly valuable source of truth. That is why God commands us to write His word on the tablet of our hearts (Proverbs 7:3) and hide the Word in our hearts (like David in Psalm 119:11). God wants His truth, not the Enemy's lies, in your heart. Take advantage of God's written Word to erase the messages and heal the wounds on your heart.

Third, talk to trusted counselors. This could mean trained psychologists, friends, mentors, parents, or even your spouse.

But this option comes with a huge warning: people will sometimes let you down. Even when they care about you, they will sometimes say and do things that are not in your best interest. Examples might be marriage counselors who tell clients they should divorce, parents who tell their adult children that they are screwups, and friends who communicate that you are not worthy of their time. In other words, be careful whom you share your wounded heart with.

In the best case, however, trusted counselors are great sources of truth. They can objectively assess situations and boldly share the truth in love. Unlike God and the Bible, they also have skin on. They can stand in front of you in a physical form that you can touch and dialogue with.

Early on in my (Shawn) healing process counselors and friends spoke truth against the lies in my heart, the messages saying I was helpless and not acceptable. Christina went out of her way to accept me as I really was, not willing to settle for the guy I was pretending to be to impress her. This kind of authentic, truthful relationship did wonders to heal my wounded heart.

Do you have trusted counselors in your life? You need people who understand biblical truth and human nature. You need people who know who you are and care about how God designed you. If they are safe to confide in, tell them about the lies and hurtful messages you have discovered on your heart. Ask them what they think the truth is. As a safeguard, take whatever they share with you to the Lord in prayer for confirmation.

Awesome job. You have identified the lies and harmful messages on your wounded heart. You have taken the next step to healing by finding out the truth. The truth is essential because it leads to freedom. "You will know the truth, and the truth will set you free" (John 8:32).

Now your actions and interactions no longer need to be guided by the lies and false messages. You are free to love your spouse secure in the knowledge that you will never be alone, that you are valuable, accepted, and good enough. Your heart, inscribed with truth, can open to allow love to flow to your spouse and those you care about. Don't stop now.

Step 3: Nurture and Care for your Heart

We're looking at the three steps necessary to move from a wounded heart to a healthy heart. First we identified the wounds and false messages. Then we replaced those messages with truth. Now we're going to see how to take good care of your heart from now on.

The wounded heart is usually covered with lies and painful messages. That is why we have to go to great lengths to get it cleaned up with the truth.

But cleanup alone is not enough. Think about it this way: cleaning up your house gives you a great feeling of satisfaction, and it is enjoyable to just sit and enjoy the clean environment. However, it does not take long for the dust to come back and the kids to clutter things up if all you do is sit and admire your handiwork. The heart is the same as your house. Spring cleaning to get the truth in there is necessary, but the heart needs more.

The wounded heart needs consistent attention and care.

The traumatic events and messages received often cause us to shut down our hearts. We end up neglecting and denying the vital center of who we are. Once neglected and shut down, the heart has only a few options.

Many people who neglect their hearts end up putting their energy into unhealthy areas to find fulfillment, meaning, and purpose. Sometimes people who neglect their hearts turn to other people to find fulfillment. They enter into codependent relationships, attempting to get all of their needs met in another person. Still other times, wounded hearts are neglected to the point that a person simply enters into long-term depression, no longer finding joy in life. In all of these cases, the damage done to a marital relationship from a neglected heart is monumental.

Again, the wounded heart needs consistent attention and care: you cannot look to others to attend to something that you are not first willing to care about. You have been given the ability to take care of your heart, even in the face of great pain.

Here are some ways to nurture your heart:

♡ Maintain a close connection with God through prayer.

♡ Write God's Word on your heart through Scripture memory.

♡ Learn to monitor whether your heart is open or closed.

♡ Notice your feelings throughout the day.

♡ Identify your feelings—give your heart a voice.

♡ Learn to validate your own feelings—they're a great source of information.

♡ Show compassion and curiosity around your heart instead of stuffing or judging your feelings ("I wonder why I am feeling that").

♡ Learn to manage your emotions (e.g., pray, breathe, stretch, listen to music, exercise, talk, etc.).

♡ Keep short accounts by lovingly confronting others when you are hurt instead of ignoring the issue (speaking the truth in love).

♡ Be quick to forgive so you don't hold on to resentment and bitterness.

♡ Find healthy relationships with people who are trustworthy so you can open your heart.

♡ Journal your feelings. Research says that when you write something down, your body doesn't have to remember it. It's like when you go to the store with a shopping list. If you write down what you need, you won't have to constantly review the list in your mind.

♡ Add laughter to your life (tell jokes and funny stories, watch comedy shows and movies).

♡ Be more aware of your likes and dislikes.

♡ Talk with trusted people about heart-level issues.

♡ Accept compliments and affirmations. It's okay to receive it when others praise you.

♡ Instead of using the clock to decide when you are hungry or tired, notice how your body feels ("I feel tired, I'm going to bed" or "I feel hungry, I'm going to eat").

♡ Recognize your natural strengths and growth areas.

♡ Keep balance in your life ("play and work; be responsible and a goof-off").

♡ Nurture healthy relationships and friendships and say "no" to unhealthy ones.

♡ Learn to set boundaries. A boundary is anything that you do in order to keep your heart open. For example, it's never okay for someone to share their feelings at your expense.

♡ Make sure your personality strengths do not get out of balance and become a weakness (i.e., too much extroversion will make you seem overwhelming to people; too much perfectionism will make you seem rigid to others).

All of these suggestions are designed to help you pay attention to your heart. That is what Proverbs 4:23 is telling us: pay close attention and protect your heart. If you have children, think back to when you held that precious child for the first time. He was so valuable and so vulnerable. You vowed to care for him, pay attention to him, protect him, and nurture him.

Can you make that same vow to your heart? You deserve it.

THE WOUNDED HEART IN MARRIAGE

This chapter has focused a lot on the individual heart, but hopefully you can see that tending to the wounded heart has huge implications for marriage. Let's conclude by taking a look at what the wounded heart does to a marital relationship, because those wounds and messages don't just affect us personally; they have a profound impact relationally.

The four couples in a recent intensive I led are great examples of the effects of early wounds:

- ♡ Couple 1—The husband's early message that he was a failure led him to work long hours to try to overcome his fear of failure. But the long hours away from home had a huge impact on his marriage. His wife longed for more intimacy and connection, not just more money.
- ♡ Couple 2—The wife feared she was not worthy, so she sought value in her children. She tried to be

supermom and even came close to pulling it off. But her efforts left her exhausted, and her husband felt neglected and uncared for.

♡ Couple 3—The wife, led by fears of not being good enough and the lie that she was alone, turned outside the marriage for some attention. Ultimately, this attention crossed the line and became an affair.

♡ Couple 4—The wife bumped up next to the walls of her husband's closed heart, begging him to open. This went on for more than twenty years. Finally, she gave up and shut down her heart. Suddenly aware of what he was losing, the husband found his heart and desired to connect with his wife. But she had already checked out, shut down for good, no longer interested in the battle. He really had changed, healed, and opened his heart. But she said it was too late.

The wounded heart leads to unhealthy choices and closed hearts. Closed hearts are near death to a marriage. Don't let any of the above scenarios be your marriage. Understand the messages on your heart, get the truth to them, and nurture this vital part of who you are.

From this healthy place, open your heart to your spouse. If your spouse follows the same process, you are in for a dynamic connection like most marriages never get to see. Wholeheartedly engaged, the healthy heart is free to open, connect to God, and pass His love and blessings on to others.

Chapter 4
The Fearful Heart

[Adam] answered, "I heard you in the garden, and I was afraid."

—Genesis 3:10

Safe Haven. n. A trustworthy person to whom you can turn, knowing that person will be emotionally available and will respond to you in a caring manner.

—Archibald Hart and Sharon Hart Morris

YOU HAVE now spent some time seeking God's amazing truth to dispel the lies that have been written on your heart. As you learned in the previous chapter, a wounded heart leads to unhealthy choices and a closed heart. The more truth God speaks into your heart, the more open and wholeheartedly engaged you become in life and in your marriage. The healthy heart is thus free to open, connect to God, and pass His love and blessings on to others.

Let's continue to identify and counteract the forces working to disconnect you from your heart and that ultimately will keep you from a wholehearted marriage. Now that you under-stand the wounded heart, let's turn our attention to the *fearful* heart.

FEAR AND SHAME IN MARRIAGE

Tonight Pastor Hodges will begin a six-part series on the Book of Genesis. Were Adam and Eve really naked in the Garden? Come see for yourself.

The above teaser headline was actually printed in a church bulletin. I (Greg) have no idea what was going on in that church, but I'm sure Pastor Hodges took a lot of grief for many months thereafter. However, I bet it was the most attended Sunday-night service in the history of that church!

Apparently this humiliated pastor had been intending to preach from Genesis 2:25, which is one of my (favorite) verses. And it has nothing to do with sex! Instead, this verse paints an amazing picture of marriage: "The man and his wife were both naked, and they felt no shame."

How cool is that? When you stand "naked" in the presence of your spouse, you have no way to hide, disguise, or conceal yourself or who you really are. You are completely exposed. In paradise Adam and Eve, husband and wife, were open and vul-nerable (naked) and yet experienced no humiliation—they felt completely safe with each other.

And yet paradise didn't last very long. Unfortunately, sin en-tered the world, and this husband and wife went through a major relationship change. Instead of feeling safe and open, suddenly they felt fear.

Contrary to what many people think, the opposite of love is not hate—it's fear. And fear is what erodes trust, openness, and vulnerability. Fear makes a marriage feel *unsafe*. Just look at what happened to Adam and Eve:

> The eyes of both of them were opened, and they realized they were naked; so they sewed fig leaves together and made coverings for themselves.
>
> Then the man and his wife heard the sound of the LORD God as he was walking in the garden in the cool of the day, and they hid from the LORD God among the trees of the garden. But the LORD God called to the man, "Where are you?"
>
> He answered, "I heard you in the garden, and I was afraid because I was naked; so I hid."
>
> And he said, "Who told you that you were naked? Have you eaten from the tree that I commanded you not to eat from?"
>
> The man said, "The woman you put here with me— she gave me some fruit from the tree, and I ate it."
>
> Then the LORD God said to the woman, "What is this you have done?"
>
> The woman said, "The serpent deceived me, and I ate." (Genesis 3:7–13)

Fear took a major toll on their marriage. All of a sudden, they realized they were naked. They felt shame. The shame caused them to cover up, conceal, disguise, and mask who they were. Worse, they went into hiding relationally. When couples cover up and hide, they suppress, shut down, and withhold from the other. And then they turn on each other.

Adam and Eve went from the security of the Garden to blaming: "The woman you put here with me—she gave me the fruit." And just like that, the perfect marriage, this unspoiled union between a husband and wife, where they were naked and unashamed, changed into something in which they were shutting down and turning on each other. Sound familiar?

What caused this unfortunate metamorphosis? The easy answer is sin. Or fear. But we want to suggest that something else entered into Adam and Eve's relationship that day they disobeyed God and ate the fruit. For the first time since they were created and were joined together as husband and wife, they felt *unsafe*.

I DON'T FEEL EMOTIONALLY SAFE

Safety is integral to everything we do. But usually when we think of safety, we think about physical safety and wellness. Physical safety in a marriage is crucial; there is no question about that. However, feeling safe is not just about protection from bodily harm—feeling *emotionally* safe is also extremely important.

I first realized this when my father and I were trying to fix a refrigerator. We had taken a broken part of our refrigerator in for repair, and each time my dad called, someone made an excuse for why it wasn't fixed. When my dad finally had had enough, he gave one of the employees a huge piece of his mind.

"I've had it!" he firmly stated. "Do you think it's good for a customer to wait several extra days for a part to be fixed? Is this how you normally run things—lie to people about when they will be serviced? I'm coming down right now to pick up the part, fixed or not." After making some additional belittling comments, he slammed the phone down.

"Wow!" I said in shocked surprise, "Dad, you really let that poor guy have it!"

When we arrived at the store, we were totally confused. Not only was the part fixed, but they had been waiting several days for us to pick it up.

"What's going on here?" Dad uttered while looking at me. "Are we in the Twilight Zone or something?"

However, we soon realized Dad's mistake. After he dropped off the part, he had misplaced the store's phone number. So by accident, he looked up the wrong number and had been calling a different repair shop. The poor guy he annihilated on the phone had never had our part. No wonder he'd acted so confused.

"Dad," I said with a laugh. "Pack your bags, you're about to go on a guilt trip!"

Dad was silent as we drove to the other repair shop.

"Hello," he said to the employee, "I'm Mr. Smalley. I called a little while ago."

"Sir," the poor guy started to say, "I'm sorry but we've lost your part . . ."

I'm sure dad was tempted to go along with his story. It sounded so much better than the one he was about to tell.

"Speaking of things being lost," Dad said, trying to be funny, "I've actually lost my mind." I broke into laughter as I listened in.

"Sorry, sir," the employee said, confused. "I'm not following you."

When someone begins to eat humble pie, the sounds coming from his mouth are often very confusing.

"Never mind," Dad explained. "I was wrong to treat you so ugly when I called a few hours ago. As it turned out, I got your shop mixed up with the shop that actually had my part. They finished the work days ago, but somehow I copied down your phone number from the Yellow Pages. Pretty funny, huh?"

After several seconds of silence, Dad realized it must not be that funny.

"I'm very sorry for the way I talked to you," he said. "I apologize."

Although I'm sure the employee wanted to let him have it, he accepted his apology and we left.

As proud as I was that my dad took personal responsibility and sought forgiveness, the part I'll never forget is the look on that poor guy's face when he realized that the customer who had reamed him out and humiliated him on the phone was now standing at the counter. He looked so unsafe—not physically unsafe but emotionally unsafe. I imagine he wasn't sure what my dad was going to say or how he was going to be treated. The look on his face revealed that he was extremely nervous. Who could blame him?

Do you ever feel this way around certain people? How many relationships do you have in your life where you feel safe to open up and share your deepest feelings, thoughts, hopes, and dreams—to share who you really are? Do you feel mostly open and emotionally available in your marriage, or do you feel guarded and distant? Do you feel like part of you wants to open up but that the other part is terrified of being emotionally vulnerable—of getting hurt?

We have been designed with a deep longing to connect with others and experience relational intimacy—especially with our spouses.

Openness is actually the default setting for your heart. No state of being takes less energy to maintain than openness. It involves just being yourself and relaxing. Maintaining defenses, walls, and force fields around your heart takes tremendous energy. Simply expressing who you are and "being" does not. And yet many of us struggle with various aspects of intimacy because it means we have to be open, and openness makes us feel vulnerable. As Archibald Hart and Sharon Hart Morris explain:

> When a husband and wife love each other, they literally give their hearts to each other for safekeeping. This is such a delicate, trusting act that any violation or injury of this trust can cause the most painful of reactions. Imagine taking the very essence of your being—your heart—and placing it in the hands of your spouse. Your heart becomes your mate's to care for, safeguard, cherish, and love. This necessitates a willingness to be vulnerable and take a bold, risky step. If your partner reciprocates, you both have chosen to risk being hurt, rejected, and abandoned. Placing your heart in the hands of another is a giant step of faith. Afterward, you can only wait to see what your spouse will do with your heart. Your desire, of course, is that your spouse will be a safe haven for your heart. And that is your spouse's longing as well.[1]

When people give their spouses access to their hearts, there's no guarantee how they will behave, what they will say, or how they will use what they learn about us.

In spite of the risks, the potential benefits of a truly open and intimate relationship are numerous. Intimacy creates the ideal opportunity to love deeply and be loved, to experience a significant sense of belonging, to have the ability to make a major difference in another's life, and to have a way of fully expressing the best of who we are. Isn't this what we want to experience in our marriages?

To achieve intimacy in marriage, we typically try to create a deep connection. We invest time in learning about each other's love language and emotional needs. We talk at a deep emotional level. We enjoy a sexual relationship. We go on romantic date nights. We give gifts like flowers, cards, and boxes of chocolate. We attend relationship conferences and read marriage books. We join small groups and talk about our marriages.

Although this sounds reasonable, in reality these strategies don't always work. The reason date nights, sex, emotional communication, love languages, flowers, cards, and even chocolate (I know this one is hard to believe) often do not result in intimacy and deep connection is our fear of being emotionally vulnerable—opening our hearts—and getting hurt.

Therefore, as a way to lessen the risks involved, we come up with a whole host of strategies to keep us from being hurt:

- ♡ We may hide by constantly withdrawing from people ("You're always running away").
- ♡ We may avoid emotional situations ("You constantly avoid me").
- ♡ We may keep parts of us shut down ("You seem so guarded").
- ♡ We may maintain superficial relationships ("Our relationship seems so shallow. I never get to see the real you").
- ♡ We may use humor as a way to distract others ("You're always making jokes").
- ♡ We may put on the happy face and pretend that all is well ("You have your fake smile on again").
- ♡ We may find ways to distract ourselves ("You're such a workaholic" or "All you do is shop").
- ♡ We may deflect intimacy attempts through conflict and negative interactions ("All we ever do is fight").
- ♡ We may get angry or demanding as a way of con-

trolling ourselves, or our spouse, from our own vulnerability ("You get so angry when I try to connect").

♡ We may overly invest in the children ("You're always with the kids; you never have time for me").

♡ We may become more needy, clingy, or possessive ("I can't believe how insecure you are").

♡ We may get anxious or have panic attacks ("Why do you seem so nervous around me?").

♡ We may limit our words and not talk ("You're always so quiet").

♡ We may maintain defenses, walls, and force fields ("It's like you're inside this huge castle; I never seem to have access to your heart").

♡ We may become more irritable, cold, or sexually indifferent ("You're never in the mood").

♡ We may turn to food for comfort and support ("Are you eating again?").

♡ We may seek outside relationships ("All you do is hang out with your friends").

♡ We may project false images so that people will like and accept us ("You seem so phony").

♡ We may ignore or deny how we actually feel ("You never share your feelings").

♡ We may isolate ourselves ("It seems like you always hide out in your cave").

♡ We may become sick ("You are always so depressed").

♡ We may attempt to numb out or anesthetize our pain through drugs, alcohol, or some other addiction ("Just keep trying to drink your pain away").

♡ We may turn on and punish ourselves ("You always beat yourself up").

♡ We may become bitter and resentful ("You seem to resent that you married me").

♡ We may get involved in an affair ("You were the last person I thought would ever be unfaithful").

♡ We may rely only on ourselves ("You're so self-reliant; you don't seem to need me").

This is why a lack of desire to connect—or an avoidance of intimacy in general—is usually about attempting to avoid being hurt. Which one(s) do you use to avoid being vulnerable or opening your heart? Unfortunately, these coping strategies require significant energy and usually limit the quality of the intimacy in your relationship, because it's hard for anyone to get close to you when you're on the other side of a thick emotional wall.

In spite of the obvious risks, how do you learn to open your heart and foster a deep connection with your spouse?

FOCUS ON CREATING A SAFE ENVIRONMENT

In terms of intimacy, the best approach is to focus significant time, attention, and energy on creating an environment that feels safe. We're not talking physical safety. We're talking emotional safety—in which all parties feel safe to truly open up and be known at a deep, intimate level.

In order for intimacy and deep connection to occur, hearts must be open. Thus, the foundation of a wholehearted marriage is feeling safe physically, intellectually, spiritually, *and* emotionally.

When people feel safe, they are naturally inclined to open their hearts. Intimacy then occurs effortlessly and naturally. In its most basic sense, intimacy is the experience of being close to another person and openly sharing something with them. This may or may not include words. It doesn't necessarily require work or effort.

The mistake many couples make—knowing they want to experience intimacy and that openness is required—is to focus on trying to be open or create intimacy. The better approach to intimacy is to focus on creating a safe environment for yourself and your spouse.

For example, when you have been hurt by your spouse, you might feel closed, shut down, or disconnected. But have you ever noticed that when he takes responsibility for his actions and seeks forgiveness, how quickly your heart opens back up? You instantly go from feeling closed to feeling connected and open.

This is because openness is the default setting of our hearts. Our hearts were designed to be open. It's all that other stuff— lies, negative messages, and hurtful behavior—that keeps our hearts shut down. But this isn't how God created us.

We have found that the only way to enjoy a close, open, intimate marital relationship is to create a safe environment where two people who want to stay in love and harmony feel very safe with each other. Emotional safety will help you create a climate in which you can build open relationships that will grow and flourish. It will help you build relationships in which you and the other person will feel cherished, honored, and alive. It's almost as if this sets a soothing tone that will allow you to feel relaxed in your relationships.

If that sounds like paradise, it's maybe because Eden was a completely safe place. Adam and Eve felt no fear there. Before they sinned, they enjoyed an amazingly intimate relationship with God and each other. They felt so close to each other that God described them as "naked without shame" and "united as one" (Genesis 2:24–25, author paraphrase). Nothing came between Adam and Eve—not insecurities, not lies written on their hearts, not sharp differences of opinion, not even clothes! They were completely open with each other—no walls, no masks, no fear. Their relationship blossomed because they felt *safe*.

In your quest to have a wholehearted marriage, make creating safety in your marriage a top priority. It must be the foundation. The only way you can intertwine your hearts together and become one is to feel safe.

Start this process by answering some basic questions:

1. Is your marriage a safe haven right now?
2. Can you trust your spouse with the deepest parts of your heart?
3. On a scale of 0–10 (with 10 being the most safe), how safe is your marriage for you? For your spouse?
4. How do you react when you feel unsafe?
5. If your marriage feels unsafe for either you or your spouse or both, how has it become that way?
6. How do you damage the safety of your marital environment?

The good news is that you can create an open atmosphere in your marriage that will allow both spouses to be their true selves. But the focus must be on creating safety.

WHAT DOES EMOTIONAL SAFETY MEAN?

Most marriage books want to coach you to use a new therapy technique, to unpack some new bit of research, or to teach you the latest five steps or seven principles. But the latest or newest keys to successful relationships won't give you what you most desire: to feel loved, close, valued, respected, cherished, and deeply connected. To experience these things requires that you feel safe with each other.

But what do we mean by feeling safe?

I asked more than one thousand couples at a recent marriage seminar to define emotional safety. Listen to some of their responses:

♡ feeling completely secure
♡ knowing that you are loved
♡ feeling accepted for who you are
♡ feeling relaxed and less tense
♡ feeling cared for above anyone else
♡ feeling free to express who you really are
♡ being loved unconditionally
♡ feeling confident and less insecure
♡ feeling respected
♡ feeling like the other person is trustworthy
♡ feeling comfortable around that person
♡ feeling like the other person will be there for me
♡ being fully understood
♡ feeling valued and honored
♡ feeling loving reassurance
♡ feeling the deep sense that the relationship is solid

♡ allowing ourselves to open fully to give and receive
love
♡ feeling like I'm not being judged
♡ feeling like the other person sees me for who I am
♡ feeling like the other person accepts my flaws as
part of the whole package
♡ feeling an atmosphere of open communication

That's a pretty amazing list, isn't it? Wouldn't it feel wonderful to have these things as the foundation of your marital relationship? Feeling emotionally safe is vital for the marriage relationship to flourish. As one author put it:

> One of our most basic needs in an intimate relationship
> is the need to feel safe. I'm not talking about physical
> safety, but rather the feeling of emotional safety. It is the
> deep sense that the relationship is solid, that our partner's
> affections are serious and committed, that we can trust
> the love we feel, and thus allow ourselves to open fully to
> give and receive it. This emotional safety is the key that
> unlocks a person's heart and soul. When we feel safe, we
> are able to open up. When we feel safe, we are able to
> risk. When we feel safe, we are able to relax. When we
> feel safe, we are able to shine.[2]

So what is emotional safety? We define emotional safety as *feeling free to open up and reveal who you really are and know that the other person will still love, understand, accept, and value you—no matter what.*

You feel emotionally safe with someone when you believe that he or she will handle your heart—your deepest feelings and desires—with genuine interest, curiosity, and care. In other words, you hold your heart out to the person and say, "Here is who I am emotionally, psychologically, spiritually, and mentally. I want you to know my heart and soul. I want you to get to know who I am and appreciate who I am and value who I am. I am a very fascinating person who will take you more than one lifetime to understand!"

But people are not going to offer their hearts or reveal who they really are if they don't feel safe.

YOUR HEART IS LIKE A SOW BUG

Have you ever been outside and noticed the sow bugs or roly-poly bugs? They are fascinating little creatures. They are silver, gray-looking little bugs that roll up into a ball when they are touched. We have them all over here in the Ozarks.

One day, Taylor (who was one at the time) was playing with me in the backyard when she discovered a nest of sow bugs. They were everywhere! She was so fascinated by how whenever she touched the bugs they would roll up into little balls. Since Taylor loves anything round, she kept flicking the bugs and squealing, "Ball . . . ball!"

Something caught my attention, and I turned away for just a moment. When I turned back toward Taylor, I was horrified to see several sow bugs rolling around in her mouth. With her mouth full, Taylor was pointing at the remaining bugs on the ground and shrieking, "Bawl . . . bawl!"

I quickly did the finger sweep and rushed her inside. Since dads usually get blamed for these things, when we reached Erin, I knew I was in big trouble. Unfortunately for me, the only thing that came to mind was: "At least she got plenty of protein!" No wonder the average mother gets nervous when leaving the kids with their father.

You might be wondering what this story has to do with safety. Actually, more than you may realize.

Before Taylor started playing, the bugs were completely open and vulnerable. But when she started flicking them, they felt threatened. In response to feeling threatened and unsafe, the bugs closed up into tight balls. And have you ever tried to get one to open up, once it has rolled into its safety ball? It is impossible, and I suspect that if you were to manage to pry it open, the bug would die.

This is exactly what our hearts do. When we feel threatened or hurt, our hearts do the same thing as the sow bug—they shut down because we don't feel safe in the situation or environment. This creates disconnection in relationships. And forcing the heart open can cause terrible damage.

While there are probably hundreds of ways to offend, frustrate, and hurt each other—causing our hearts to shut down—we consistently see several that top the list. We actually asked those same one thousand couples at a marriage seminar this question: "What makes you feel unsafe in your marriage?" We weren't sure what would emerge as number one, but one behavior stood out above all the rest: criticism.

I've heard it said that a psychologist is a person who will give you expensive advice that your wife will give you for free. Criticism, like your spouse's free advice, is like pollution in a marriage. Critical words are like contamination that spreads throughout the relationship and kills intimacy and connection.

Criticism is when we express our disapproval by pointing out someone's faults or shortcomings in a hurtful manner. When we criticize, we sit in judgment over our spouses. Criticism is always about getting someone to do something we want. We may want something or feel responsible for our partner's behavior, so we attempt to force him or her into submission. Criticism erodes the loving trust that keeps couples together. It wears us down and creates defensiveness and anger.

Here are some other things that make the relationship feel unsafe:

- ♡ being physically abused, threatened, or intimidated
- ♡ feeling belittled
- ♡ having a spouse withdraw (and never return) during an argument or tense situation
- ♡ receiving hurtful jokes or sarcastic comments at your expense
- ♡ feeling defensiveness
- ♡ having your feelings, thoughts, beliefs, and opinions judged
- ♡ being ignored or minimized
- ♡ feeling or receiving anger
- ♡ having someone attempt to control you
- ♡ being yelled at or spoken to with harsh words
- ♡ receiving broken promises
- ♡ receiving constant nagging
- ♡ being the center of gossip or having private information shared without your blessing (your confidence is betrayed)
- ♡ having the past brought up over and over
- ♡ having someone not listen to you or seem to be uninterested
- ♡ being rejected or abandoned

♡ having negative assumptions or conclusions made about you, and you not getting the benefit of the doubt

♡ experiencing deception

♡ being disrespected or dishonored

♡ having your spouse not share his or her feelings or open up emotionally

♡ being teased

♡ feeling affection or sex is being withheld or used as a weapon

♡ being betrayed

♡ feeling like your opinions don't matter

♡ being verbally attacked

♡ having someone not take personal responsibility and be unwilling to admit when he or she is wrong

♡ being forced to do something you're uncomfortable with

♡ having your spouse try to fix you or solve the problem

♡ feeling unforgiveness

♡ being embarrassed or humiliated in front of others

♡ having your needs dismissed as unimportant

♡ being taken for granted or unappreciated

Which behaviors do you especially feel unsafe around? Do you behave in ways that, even unintentionally, result in your spouse's feeling unsafe?

When you encounter these behaviors, your heart will shut down. It may not close up completely, but it definitely takes its toll on the marriage. And you may remember from a previous chapter that when your heart closes, you don't feel love for your spouse because you also shut off God's love from flowing through you.

This is why keeping two hearts open to each other is so important. We need God's love constantly flowing between us. Otherwise we won't feel love and can't live out the Greatest Commandment (love God, self, and others). We will never have the type of marriage we long for.

MAKING YOUR MARRIAGE FEEL LIKE THE SAFEST PLACE ON EARTH

What can you do to help your spouse feel safe? This process involves an attitude and an action:

- ♡ Attitude—Recognize your mate's value.
- ♡ Action—Treat your mate in valuable ways.

Attitude

People feel emotionally safe when they believe the other person gets how valuable and vulnerable they are. We call this *honor*. By honor we mean a simple decision to place high value, worth, and importance on another person by viewing him or her as a priceless gift and granting him or her a position in your life worthy of great respect.

Honor is a gift we give to others. It isn't purchased by their actions or contingent on our emotions. You're giving them distinction whether or not they like it, want it, or deserve it. You just do it; it's a decision you make.

However, we live in a society that aggressively promotes the opposite of honor. Our culture promotes selfishness, an attitude of "I'm going to look out for myself."

One of the most tragic examples of this self-focus is an incident when a surveillance camera captured footage of a seventy-eight-year-old man trying to cross a street in Hartford, Connecticut. Millions of people on YouTube have watched in horror as the man steps off the curb and two cars that are racing approach him. The first car swerves around the man. The second car hits him, throwing him high into the air like a doll, and then speeds away.

What followed is even more chilling: people walked by and did nothing. Nine vehicles passed him lying in the street. Some drivers slowed down to look but drove on. The man ended up lying in the street for several minutes before a police car arrived. It's like you're watching the parable of the good samaritan played out. But a samaritan never shows up.

"This is a clear indication of what we have become," Hartford police chief Daryl K. Roberts said at a news conference, "when you see a man lying in the street, hit by a car, and people drive around him and walk by him. At the end of the day, it seems that we have little regard for each other." Police later reported receiving four 911 calls, but still, no one stooped to hold this dying man's hand until help came.[3]

Honor is about kindness, compassion, gentleness, sensitivity, and acting in loving ways. This is God's heart, as He makes clear in 1 Corinthians 12:24–26: "God has so composed the body . . . that the members may have the same care for one another. If one member suffers, all suffer together; if one member is honored, all rejoice together" (ESV).

A little nine-year-old boy from China, Lin Hao, lived his life by this verse, though he may not have been aware of it. He was an honorary flag bearer in the 2008 Olympics for his heroics. This little boy was in a school that collapsed during the Sichuan, China, earthquake that killed more than seventy thousand people. Twenty of the boy's classmates died in the terrible disaster. Miraculously, somehow he freed himself from the rubble and then returned to free two more of his classmates.

When he was asked why he did so, this precious young man said, "I'm the hall monitor. It's my job." What an amazing little boy. What a great testimony of honor.

The apostle Paul encouraged the early Christians to honor one another: "Be devoted to one another in brotherly love; give preference to one another in honor" (Romans 12:10 NASB). The definition of *honor* we prefer is "to give preference to someone by attaching high value to him." Honor has to be the center of a marriage, and it is not a difficult practice to master. Honor in action gives legs to the words "I love you."

But understand something extremely important: honor will take place only if your heart is open. It's impossible to honor anyone—including yourself—when your heart is shut down.

Action

People feel emotionally safe when they experience someone treating them in valuable ways, when that person handles their hearts (their deepest feelings, thoughts, and desires) with genuine interest, curiosity, honor, and care.

I (Shawn) was sitting in my office talking with a colleague when I heard a faint knock on the door. I rolled my chair over (my office was pretty small) and cracked the door open to peer outside. There before me stood my six-year-old daughter, Taylor.

Something was definitely wrong, her face was covered with

blood, and her shirt was torn. Despite her traumatic appearance, Taylor had a really peaceful look on her face (she may have been in shock). Everything inside me wanted to freak out, but Taylor's calm demeanor told me I should try to stay even-keeled.

I gently asked, "What happened, baby?"

She responded, "I was riding my bike down the big hill when I must have hit a rock. The next thing I know, I was flying over the handle bars and skidding on the pavement."

She had walked half a mile pushing her bike (she is her father's responsible child) to get to my office. She went on to explain how she had to hide behind trees when cars passed because she was afraid of what she looked like.

"Does it hurt?" I asked. Remember, I am a psychologist, not the kind of doctor who actually helps in medical situations like this.

She was obviously in pain, and I needed to see exactly how bad she was hurt. I carried her to the bathroom (surely Christina would not be mad about blood stains on my shirt if they came from our daughter) and began washing her up.

After a few seconds, Taylor looked up at me and said, "Dad, can you just hold me?"

I picked her up, and she nestled into my chest. And for the first time since the crash, Taylor allowed herself to cry. She wept uncontrollably.

After a few minutes, she had regained her composure, and I set her back down. "Why did you walk so far to get to me?" I asked.

She looked up at me with her big blue eyes and said, "I found you because you make me feel safe when I get scared."

That's honor in action.

If you want to make your marriage feel like the safest place on earth, you must not only pledge to see your mate as valuable, you must be able to convey that honor through your words, actions, and deeds. At a recent marriage seminar, I (Greg) asked more than one thousand couples what their spouses do to help them feel emotionally safe. Listen to their words. "I feel safe when you:

- ♡ pray for me
- ♡ help challenge the lies written on my heart
- ♡ keep track of my positive behavior—try to notice what I do that pleases you
- ♡ list all the things you admire about me (my personality traits, appearance, thinking patterns, gender differences, faith patterns, shared values, parenting skills, concerns, opinions, and life goals)
- ♡ don't judge my feelings, innermost thoughts, needs, and desires
- ♡ love and accept me unconditionally
- ♡ accept my influence (when you're teachable)
- ♡ express your love and appreciation with words
- ♡ practice healthy communication
- ♡ have the best interest of our relationship foremost in your mind
- ♡ are not self-centered or selfish
- ♡ don't intentionally hurt me
- ♡ give me your full attention when I talk
- ♡ allow me to enter into your inner world—share your feelings, thoughts, fears, insecurities, flaws, and weaknesses
- ♡ learn to be a great listener—when you show genuine interest in what I say
- ♡ validate my feelings
- ♡ are approachable

♡ pray with me

♡ reassure me of your love

♡ consider my point of view

♡ are trustworthy

♡ act curious about me

♡ provide affection and not just before sex (women . . . sometimes we men just want to be held and all you want is sex—we are not just a piece of meat!)

♡ spend time with me

♡ constructively resolve our conflict and arguments

♡ serve me in ways that are meaningful to me

♡ are honest and tell the truth

♡ provide positive affirmation

♡ have fun and laugh with me

♡ honor my boundaries

♡ keep private the things I share with you in confidence."

Now it's your turn. You and your spouse look at each other and take turns completing this statement: "I feel safe when you . . ."

Use the above list as well as your own answers to find out what makes you feel safe with each other. All of these suggestions are designed to help you create a marriage that feels like the safest place on earth. That is what 1 Peter 1:22 is telling us: "Love one another deeply, from the heart."

But what if your spouse's heart remains shut down?

THE WALLED-UP HEART

"You've filled in this application all right except for one thing, Mr. Perkins," the insurance salesman said to his customer. "Where it asks the relationship of Mrs. Perkins to yourself, you should have put down 'wife,' not 'strained.'"

When a marriage is strained, often one or both spouses shut down and erect a wall around their hearts. You may have a mate who seems to erect walls toward most people. Your spouse may have come from an abused background and have a general distrust toward everyone.

People build walls in response to a perceived threat or when they feel unsafe. Although an emotional wall may keep the individual out of harm's way, the spouse usually experiences the wall as an obstacle that stands in the way of achieving intimacy and connection. None of us likes a relational wall. It keeps us from feeling close to the other person.

When I (Greg) encounter a wall separating me from Erin, my natural reaction is to think, *I have to destroy her walls. I have to break them down and get past the walls that stand in my way.* So I attempt to tear down, bust through, dig under, or climb over the wall. It seems like the only reasonable thing to do—something is in my way, so I'll get rid of it. However, as logical as this sounds, it has the unfortunate effect of making things worse.

So before you head toward the wall with a sledgehammer, think about why that wall got erected in the first place. Walls are built by people who feel threatened. Behind every wall we find a person who feels unsafe. So as soon as the jackhammers come out or the bulldozers show up, you confirm to that person that you are a dangerous threat.

When you take someone who already feels unsafe and you start trying to break down his or her emotional walls, the person feels a greater sense of threat. Instead of achieving the intimacy and connection you're wanting, what you'll end up with is a thicker wall. The person will work that much harder to maintain the defenses to keep you away. The wall gets thicker and higher, guard dogs show up to patrol the perimeter, and razor-sharp barbed-wire fence gets coiled on top.

Any time you try to break through someone's emotional barrier, you're doing what we call "dishonoring his or her walls." And this never has a happy ending for the relationship.

The alternative is to honor the walls and care about the feelings of the person behind the fortress. It will help you to recognize that people erect walls only when they feel unsafe. If you understand that, anytime you encounter a wall, you can know that the person behind the wall feels unsafe, and you can choose to care more about that person and those feelings than getting what you want. It is generally even irrelevant whether or not the perceived threat is real or imagined. Just the fact that the person *feels* unsafe should matter to you.

If you determine that you are willing to do whatever it takes to prevent your spouse from feeling more unsafe, and that you instead want to find ways to care about and protect the individual behind the wall, and if you really follow through on that, you will find that that person will generally lay the wall down in time. It takes a lot of energy to maintain walls and fortresses, after all, and most people would rather use that energy to live and love and have good, safe, satisfying, intimate relationships.

Erin and I learned about protective walls early in our marriage. For the first few years I kept some money hidden from Erin. We seemed to always fight about money and how we were going to spend it. I finally got so tired of feeling controlled that any time I made some extra money, I would keep some of it back.

Occasionally I would use the cash to buy antiques or something else I wanted.

One day an antique dealer with great sporting items called the house and told Erin, "I have a neat item for Greg."

"That's great. I want to get him a present," she replied. "What is it?"

The man described an old laced leather basketball, something Erin knew I would love.

"Yes, I'll take it!" she said excitedly.

When the dealer called back the next day, I picked up the phone. Erin hadn't told the dealer that she wanted to surprise me with the basketball, so the man told me all about it, never mentioning his conversation with Erin. I quickly hopped in the car to meet the dealer and buy the ball, using my secret stash of money.

The following day Erin called the man. "Can we meet so I can get the basketball?"

"Actually," he replied, "your husband already came by yesterday to buy the ball."

Not only was Erin disappointed that she couldn't surprise me with the basketball, she was puzzled about where I had gotten the money without her knowing about it. She visited the bank, and when she found no withdrawal, she started getting suspicious. She confronted me with her suspicions, and I finally admitted my secret stash.

As you can imagine, my deception deeply hurt Erin. It made it difficult for her to trust me on financial matters. She'd wanted to surprise me with a gift, but instead she was the one who had been surprised by my duplicity. She erected a thick wall between us to protect herself from other possible deceptions.

I cannot tell you how frustrating this situation was for me. Things would be going great, and then Erin would come at me with receipts and demand, "What are you doing? What's going on?" I continually tried to knock down her walls. I bullied her and tried to strong-arm her into dropping the matter and just trust me. The more I hedged, the more Erin distrusted. It was a vicious cycle.

Nothing improved until we got some coaching from one of my mentors, Dr. Gary J. Oliver. When I described our struggle, Gary said, "Greg, you need to honor the fact that Erin needs this wall up right now. Your deception threatened her. She doesn't feel safe. You have to seek to understand her and value her concerns."

I was shocked. I just knew that Gary was going to tell Erin that it was a one-time mistake, that she should relax and trust me.

"But Gary," I said, "I made one little mistake. She's acting like I had an affair or something. Her walls are killing our marriage."

"I understand that the wall doesn't help build your relationship," Gary said. "At some point, if your marriage is going to flourish, Erin's walls will need to come down. But let them be okay for now. Honor her walls."

"What does that mean?" I asked, dejected.

"Instead of trying to crash through Erin's wall, honor her need to protect herself. Instead of insisting that she just trust you, create an environment of safety. Over time, Erin will feel safe enough to take down the wall and trust you again."

Gary gave me some amazing encouragement that day. First, Erin needed to know that I understood the wall was there for a reason and that I accepted its presence. This was "honoring her wall." I didn't like Erin's wall, but I understood that hiding money from her resulted in her not trusting me. I had to get Erin to feel that her emotional well-being was important to me. I remember telling her that her walls could stay up as long as she needed them—that I would no longer try to get her to trust me.

Second, I let Erin know that I was no longer going to convince her to be open with me or tear down her walls until she felt safe. It was *her* heart, and she would get to decide when she felt safe enough to trust me. My job was to give Erin every reason in the world to feel safe with me, while still honoring her right and responsibility to take care of herself.

I imagined stationing myself as a sentry outside her heart. I told Erin, "I understand that the wall is there because I made you feel unsafe. And I want you to know that I am going to stand outside this wall as a guard and work on me so that you can eventually feel safe. I'll try to keep my mouth shut and start discovering other things I've done to create such an unsafe place for you. I won't rest until you finally feel relaxed to open up and be yourself around me. I'll even try to protect you from others who try to convince you to open up to me."

Respect and honor your spouse's wall. He or she has built it for a reason. And when you create a safe environment in your marriage, when your spouse no longer needs to protect herself from you, the wall will eventually come down.

To have a foundation of safety built into a marriage, especially emotionally, makes opening up significantly easier. And that truly is the antidote for a fearful heart. When you and your spouse know that both of you are committed to creating a safe marriage, you will avoid things that would cause hurt in either of you, and you will begin building a strong foundation for a whole-hearted marriage.

Your home should feel like the safest place on earth.

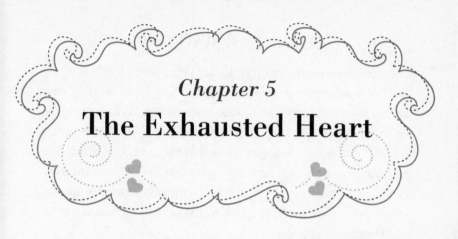

Chapter 5
The Exhausted Heart

*These people honor me with their lips, but their hearts
are far from me.*

—Matthew 15:8

*Overcommitment and exhaustion are the most insidious
and pervasive marriage killers you will ever encounter
as a couple.*

—James Dobson

WHOLEHEARTED MARRIAGE is the goal. We have seen how
wounded and fearful hearts negatively impact marriage
because they close down and block the flow of love. A third force
attacking the heart is the hectic pace of our lives, which ultimately
leads to exhaustion.

The exhausted heart may be open or closed, but its impact on
marriage is dangerous either way. The exhausted heart is harmful
to marriage because there is nothing in it to give to a spouse. Use
this chapter to see if you fit the diagnosis for an exhausted heart;
and if so, determine how to get back on track.

STOP THE MADNESS

Sometimes we need to stop and ask, "What in the world is going on?" We are moving at an ever-increasing speed toward who knows where and at a cost of who knows what. Well, actually we do know some of the cost . . . our relationships. As life gets faster, busier, more frenzied, and more hectic, our marriages suffer. We just don't have enough time for each other. And if we somehow carve out some time, we don't have any energy. Our valuable, vulnerable hearts are run ragged, worn out, and exhausted.

Here's a sample day:

- ♡ 5:45 a.m. Becky wakes up and hits the streets for her morning run (got to keep that girlish figure).
- ♡ 6:15 a.m. Jim gets out of bed and heads for the coffee.
- ♡ 6:45 a.m. Time to shake the three kids from slumber.
- ♡ 7:00 a.m. Jim jumps into the car (one-hour commute with traffic), headed for work; Becky breaks up a fight between her eight- and six-year-olds.
- ♡ 7:02 a.m. Becky wrestles clothes onto her four-year-old, who still has sleep in her eyes.
- ♡ 7:10 a.m. Kids sit down at the bar for Pop-Tarts and cereal; Becky opts for a protein bar.
- ♡ 7:20 a.m. Becky and kids in the car for school and daycare.
- ♡ 7:22 a.m. Someone notices that the four-year-old never made it into the car; Becky turns around to pick her up.
- ♡ 8:00 a.m. Becky stares at her class full of third

graders; she is already tired; Jim starts his day at the construction company.

♡ 8:01 a.m. to 4:00 p.m. Becky has tests to grade, students to teach, discipline issues to handle, two phone calls to parents, one committee meeting, and bus duty to monitor.

♡ 8:01 a.m. to 6:00 p.m. Jim has to locate and motivate subcontractors, consult with architects, straighten out paychecks with the timekeeper, defend their schedule with the owner, and listen to one employee's marital problems.

♡ 4:30 p.m. Becky rounds up the last of her kids from daycare, leaving just enough time to grab them some snacks.

♡ 5:33 p.m. Becky gets her eight-year-old to baseball practice (almost on time).

♡ 6:00 p.m. Jim leaves work ready to face the rush hour that has no rush.

♡ 6:02 p.m. Becky gets the six-year-old to ballet (closer to on time).

♡ 6:05 p.m. Becky and Jim talk on their cell phones to coordinate Jim's pickup at baseball practice.

♡ 6:58 p.m. Wreck on the freeway has cost Jim some time. Jim calls the baseball coach to make sure someone can stay with his son until he makes it there for pickup.

♡ 7:00 p.m. Becky picks up child from ballet and heads for Chick-fil-A to grab dinner to go.

♡ 7:12 p.m. Jim picks up the eight-year-old from baseball.

♡ 7:40 p.m. Jim eats his sandwich; eight-year-old

not hungry; other two kids already ate in the car;
Becky is wrestling them into the shower.

♡ 8:10 p.m. Jim takes over kid duty—getting teeth
brushed and heads in beds.

♡ 8:15 p.m. Becky grabs a few bites of food before
heading to the shower herself.

♡ 8:30 p.m. Jim dozes off while reading the paper.

♡ 9:00 p.m. Becky watches a little HGTV to un-
wind.

♡ 10:30 p.m. Becky heads to bed.

♡ 11:00 p.m. Jim finds his way to bed.

What are your observations as you read through this list?
Look busy? Nothing compared to your life? Chances are this is
pretty close to most of our lives. It is a pretty typical day in the
life of a married couple in the United States. It's the American
dream: good jobs, nice home, active kids, concerned parents. But
take a closer look . . . what is missing?

You could find lots of things, but one thing in particular
jumps out at me as a marriage counselor. There is absolutely no
connection time between Becky and Jim. No chance for them to
share, laugh, love, or play together. The little time at the end of
the day that they could have together is not utilized for connection. How could it be? They are exhausted.

It was not supposed to be this way. Futurists (cool name for
people who study the future) in the early and mid-1900s were
predicting that the speed of our progress and advancements
would have amazing consequences. The major concern was that
we would have so much leisure time that we would not know
what to do with ourselves. Testimony before a 1967 Senate sub-
committee claimed that by 1985 people could be working just
twenty-two hours a week or twenty-seven weeks a year.[1]

Wouldn't that be a nice schedule? But it was not the case in 1985, and it is certainly not true today. Do you know anyone over the age of twelve who has a problem with too much spare time? I don't. Even my retired parents have so much going on at the ranch that I have a hard time getting them on the phone sometimes.

Spare time, leisure time, down time . . . these are the times when open hearts, deep connections, and successful marriages thrive. Unfortunately, these are the very things that are missing in our lives. Leisure time falls into what author Richard Swenson calls *margin*—the space between workload and our limits.

After years of deliberate study, cultural observation, and medical experience, Swenson wrote the book *Margin* to describe the state of overload and exhaustion in our country and to offer some solutions. Contrasting margin and overload, Swenson says:

Overload is fatigue; margin is energy.
Overload is hurry; margin is calm.
Overload is anxiety; margin is security.
Overload is the disease of the new millennium; margin is its cure.

Swenson goes on to list the types of overload we face: activity overload, change overload, choice overload, commitment overload, debt overload, decision overload, expectation overload, fatigue overload, hurry overload, information overload, media overload, noise overload, people overload, possession overload, technology overload, traffic overload, and work overload.[2] I got overloaded just reading the list.

Our busy lives leave no room for margin. The pace is too frantic. Every new invention is designed to speed up life—this will help you cook faster; this will help you work faster; this will make your car go faster; this will make your . . . everything makes your life go faster. But faster is not always best.

As we mentioned previously, Carl Jung said in the early 1900s, "Hurry is not of the devil, hurry is the devil." Pause for a moment and reflect upon your week. Can you remember any times when you were in a hurry? Multiple times?

Let's look at a sports analogy for a moment. I love college basketball, particularly the playoffs and the Final Four (I am still a little bitter that Greg took his son instead of me when he was invited a few years back).

There are two styles of offense in college basketball. The traditional offense is slower. In it, teams get rebounds, walk the ball up the court, set up their play, execute their cuts and screens, and gradually work toward getting a good shot. The other offense, an athletic style, could not be more different. In an athletic offense, teams get the rebound and pass the ball out quickly to the outlet man, he dribbles or throws the ball down court immediately, and the players rely on their athletic ability to score points.

Very often in big games, teams with contrasting styles of offense will inevitably get matched up to play each other. You know how it works if you like watching these big games. They tell you the game is going to start at 7:00 p.m., so you turn on the TV only to find out that the game tip-off really is not until 8:04 p.m., but until then you get to listen to people who are no longer good enough to play or coach tell you what you are going to see when the game finally does start. Still, I'm a guy, so I am obligated to watch all of this pregame.

The only part of the pregame that my wife will watch with me is when they do the special-interest story about one of the players. Typically, it goes something like, "Kevin Walls sits at the end of the bench, but he is really lucky just to be on the team.

Eight years ago, Kevin lost his little toe on his right foot in a farming accident. Kevin almost bled to death but his dog, Wooden, rushed for help." The good thing about these stories is the way they appeal to our wives. Christina will now sit and watch the entire game with me just to see if nine-toed Kevin gets any playing time.

The climactic point of the pregame is when the "experts" predict who is going to win. When teams with contrasting styles of offense play each other, the answer is always the same. The team that controls the tempo of the game will win, they say. If the athletic team gets the game going fast, it will win because of its exceptional talent. If the traditional team gets the game slowed down, it will win because of its superior ability to execute and score.

Your life is similar to college basketball in one way: whoever controls the tempo will ultimately win. By *win* we mean determine how much joy and fulfillment you find in your time here on earth. Win in terms of determining how much success you have in your marriage.

You see, the Enemy wants you to play that fast-paced, up-tempo, helter-skelter offense. He wants to run you ragged. You, on the other hand, were designed for the slowed-down, more deliberate, controlled-tempo lifestyle. We are all capable of short bursts of amazing speed and productivity, but we were designed by our heavenly Father to appreciate the health in "being still," "waiting on the Lord," and slowing down to recharge.

Who is winning the battle over the pace of your life—the Enemy or you?

The following story is floating around on the Internet. It appears to be adapted from an article called "If Satan Wanted to Capture our Attention, How Would He Do It?" written by Al Menconi?[3] Unfortunately, it could be true.

Satan called a worldwide convention of demons. In his opening address he said, "We can't keep Christians from going to church. We can't keep them from reading their Bibles and knowing the truth. We can't even keep them from forming an intimate relationship with their Savior. Once they gain that connection with Jesus, our power over them is broken. So let them go to their churches; let them have their covered dish dinners; *but* steal their time so they don't have time to develop a relationship with Jesus Christ.

"This is what I want you to do," said the devil: "distract them from gaining hold of their Savior and maintaining that vital connection throughout their day!"

"How shall we do this?" his demons shouted.

"Keep them busy in the nonessentials of life and invent innumerable schemes to occupy their minds," he answered. "Tempt them to spend, spend, spend, and borrow, borrow, borrow. Persuade the wives to go to work for long hours and the husbands to work 6–7 days each week, 10–12 hours a day, so they can afford their empty lifestyles. Keep them from spending time with their children. As their families fragment, soon their homes will offer no escape from the pressures of work!

"Overstimulate their minds so that they cannot hear that still, small voice. Entice them to play the radio or cassette player whenever they drive and to keep the TV, VCR, CDs, and their PCs going constantly in their home, and see to it that every store and restaurant in the world plays nonbiblical music constantly. This will jam their minds and break that union with Christ.

"Fill the coffee tables with magazines and newspapers. Pound their minds with the news 24 hours a day. Invade their driving moments with billboards. Flood their mail-boxes with junk mail, mail-order catalogs, sweepstakes, and every kind of newsletter and promotional offering free products, services, and false hopes.

"Keep skinny, beautiful models on the magazines and TV so the husbands will believe that outward beauty is what's important, and they'll become dissatisfied with their wives. Keep the wives too tired to love their husbands at night. Give them headaches too! If they don't give their husbands the love they need, they will begin to look elsewhere. That will fragment their families quickly!

"Give them Santa Claus to distract them from teaching their children the real meaning of Christmas. Give them an Easter bunny so they won't talk about [Jesus'] resurrection and power over sin and death.

"Even in their recreation, let them be excessive. Have them return from their recreation exhausted. Keep them too busy to go out in nature and reflect on God's creation. Send them to amusement parks, sporting events, plays, concerts, and movies instead. Keep them busy, busy, busy!

"And when they meet for spiritual fellowship, involve them in gossip and small talk so that they leave with troubled consciences. Crowd their lives with so many good causes they have no time to seek power from Jesus. Soon they will be working in their own strength, sacrificing their health and family for the good of the cause."

"It will work!" "It will work!"

It was quite a plan! The demons went eagerly to their assignments, causing Christians everywhere to get busier and more rushed, going here and there. Having little time for their God or their families. Having no time to tell others about the power of Jesus to change lives.

If this is the Enemy's plan, it often seems to be working in my life. I am not relationally at my best when I am speeding through life. Although I am certain God did not create me to frantically hurry around like a chicken with its head cut off, I seem to live most of my life this way.

I have been conditioned to rush. My dad knew only one word in Spanish when I was a kid. He would frequently yell ¡*ándale!* at my sister and me to get going and speed up. For years, I thought ¡*ándale!* meant someone is going to die if you do not pick up the pace.

I catch myself sometimes rushing my kids for no good reason. At nightly bath time you would think there was an ESPN film crew following me around documenting the NASCAR pit-crew-like precision I use in getting my kids out of dirty clothes, into the bath, scrubbed up, dried off, teeth brushed, and tucked into bed.

Unfortunately, this hurry takes its toll on their spirits. I cannot think of any loving interactions I have had with my children when I was rushing them to get somewhere or to get something done. With my heart rate elevated, my blood pressure spiking, and my tone of voice raised, I am rarely proud of the way I speak to them in these hectic moments. They deserve better.

There is a high cost for the fast pace we are living. Hectic schedules lead to hurried interactions, which lead to exhausted, empty people. Empty people have nothing to share. With nothing to share, relationships founder. Les and Leslie Parrot have spent years studying and helping couples succeed in marriage. In their book *Your Time-Starved Marriage*, they say:

Busy people rarely give their best to the ones they love. They serve leftovers—the emotions and energy that remain after one's primary attention has already been given to others. Too drained, too tired, or too preoccupied, they fail to give their loved ones the attention they deserve. And a marriage cannot survive on leftovers forever.[4]

We are a busy people serving leftovers in our marriages. Hearts are often exhausted and empty at the end of the day or on weekends when we finally get some face time with our spouses.

As is always the case, God has a solution. A verse in the book of Romans reminds us not to be conformed to this world, but rather to be transformed by the renewing of our minds (see Romans 12:2). We can continue to conform ourselves to the busy hurried pace of this world and its resulting exhaustion. Or we can transform our lives by intentionally investing ourselves in a process that will lead from exhaustion into health and fullness.

RECHARGING THE EXHAUSTED HEART

The wholehearted marriage we long for requires full engagement. Passion requires energy. Intimacy requires attention.

All these things are possible in marriage, but none of these things is possible when hearts are exhausted. The pace and demands of life are so fast and overwhelming that we end up hurried, frazzled, and empty. There are steps you can take to move from an exhausted to a healthy heart.

Step 1: Slow Down and Simplify

I (Shawn) actually just slowed down and prayed for five minutes before starting this section. The title of the section made me feel like I should. Sadly, I cannot say I have done that before every section of this book (Don't say "It shows").

The point is that it is against my natural tendency to slow down. I would definitely say that I want God to guide my steps, words, actions, life . . . but many times I don't take the time to wait on Him. In visiting with friends, family, and folks who come in for help, it is apparent that I am not alone. We all get in a hurry and miss God.

John Ortberg is one of my favorite authors. In his book *The Life You've Always Wanted*, Ortberg recalls a time when he approached his mentor, wanting to know how he could deepen his relationship with God. Ortberg's mentor replied, "You must ruthlessly eliminate hurry from your life."[5]

To improve our marriages, we must first slow down and connect with God. Remember, He is the Source of all the good things you want to experience and then pass along to your spouse. Experiencing God in an intimate way requires intentional slowing.

Author and pastor Chuck Swindoll left California to become the president of Dallas Theological Seminary. After a few years at DTS, he wrote *Intimacy with the Almighty*. When asked why he was writing a book about slowing, solitude, silence, and simplifying, Swindoll responded that his seminary students were so busy learning about God that they were missing out on a chance to actually experience relationship with God.[6]

It happens in seminary, it happens in church, it happens in homes, it happens in families, and it happens in life. We get so busy and in such a hurry that we miss out on the blessings of an intimate, connected relationship with God.

God has some really simple, time-tested formulas that will lead us into a deeper connection with Him.

- ♡ "Be still, and know that I am God" (Psalm 46:10). This one's pretty simple. How do I know God and hear His voice in this noisy, chaotic world? By being still.
- ♡ "They that wait upon the LORD shall renew their strength; they shall mount up with wings as eagles" (Isaiah 40:31, KJV). Again, pretty simple. How do I regain some strength and energy when I feel empty? By waiting upon the Lord.
- ♡ "Come to me, all you who are weary and burdened, and I [Jesus] will give you rest" (Matthew 11:28). Ah, the simplicity of it. How do we deal with the exhaustion and fatigue we are facing? By coming to Jesus.

Be still. Wait upon the Lord. Come and rest. Very simple, very practical, and very countercultural. Are you willing to go against the pull of our society in order to connect with God? Your exhausted heart is longing for it.

Slowing down and connecting with God is a start, but you need more than that. This is more than a plea for you to add a thirty-minute quiet time to your day. This is a plea to change your lifestyle. Still not sure if this message applies to you? Author and speaker Stephanie Wolfe sent me the following questions to assess the pace of one's life.

Slow Down Test

Answer 2 for "absolutely true," 1 for "somewhat true," and 0 for "not at all true."

I always eat fast.	2	1	0
I talk rapidly.	2	1	0
I often put words into other people's mouths.	2	1	0
I find it frustrating if people speak too slowly.	2	1	0
I almost always feel pressed for time.	2	1	0
I don't like to linger over a meal.	2	1	0
I often feel harried at work.	2	1	0
I often push the Close Door button on elevators.	2	1	0
I can feel my blood pressure climb in slow checkout lines.	2	1	0
I follow the car in front of me closely when driving.	2	1	0
I push the Walk button at intersections repeatedly.	2	1	0
I get very frustrated when people are late.	2	1	0
I often do two things at once to save time.	2	1	0
I get restless if I have to sit still.	2	1	0
I feel as if I'm wasting time if I do only one thing at a time.	2	1	0
I get crazy when people ahead of me are walking too slowly.	2	1	0

Scoring

A score of 24–32: Your fast ways are very likely compromising your health and well-being.

A score of 16–23: You're a borderline speedaholic. You'd enjoy life more if you dialed back a bit.

A score of 0–15: Bravo! You're taking life at a moderate pace and enjoying life as it arrives.

How did you do? Is your speed impacting the state of your heart and the amount of time and energy you have to share with others?

Slowing down to connect with God and your spouse is going to take some intentional action on your part. Benefits of this intentional action will lead you from exhausted to energized, empty to refueled, and surviving to thriving. Here are some ideas to get you started.

First, get some rest. I once heard Oprah Winfrey say, "I don't have the right to be tired." She was referencing the amount of work and hardship her ancestors went through to support her belief that she was obligated to work herself to exhaustion. Many of us have this mentality. Everyone else is working hard—getting up before sunrise, staying way past five o'clock, coming in to work on the weekends . . . not to get ahead, just to keep up—and so I have to too.

Despite what the world or Oprah would tell us, you do have a right to be tired. The healthiest (and most courageous) thing in the world that you can do is to admit it. I recently came across the following lament from a pastor, "I was born tired. I've lived tired, and if nothing changes, it looks as if I'll die tired. However, if I am still tired when I get to heaven, I'm coming straight back."[7]

We are a sleep-deprived culture. The consensus seems to be that we need eight to nine hours of sleep a night as adults, but a quick informal poll will tell you that is not happening for many people.

Dan Cathy, current CEO of Chick-fil-A restaurants, is an amazingly gifted leader. He is very busy running a "family business" that now boasts more than thirteen hundred stores. Because of the leadership demands of his position, Cathy decided that his health goal for 2008 would be to get eight hours of sleep per night. Halfway through the year, he had accomplished his goal forty-five nights. Cathy said this is the most difficult health goal he had ever set for himself (impressive for a man who has run marathons), but he will also tell you the emotional, mental, and physical benefits he feels on the days following the eight hours of sleep make it a worthwhile goal.

I'm not saying your body cannot function on fewer than eight hours of sleep. Obviously, it can. After lecturing my dad on the benefits of more sleep, he responded with, "Anybody who sleeps more than six hours a night is burning daylight." (Never mind that there is no "daylight" at 5:00 a.m. when he wakes up). I am saying that if you want to counteract some of your heart exhaustion, get more sleep. Emotionally connecting with others on a deep heart level takes more energy than most people would imagine. Get the rest you need to supply that energy.

Second, learn to say no. Our culture is not going to do you any favors in helping you slow down. It will be up to you. People will continue to demand things from you. Your kids will still want your attention—and your cooking, laundering, chauffeuring, and playing. Your boss will still want your time and energy. Your church will still want you to volunteer. Your friends will still want your counsel and guidance. Your extended family will still want your participation in their lives.

You have to learn when and where to say no. Women in particular find this difficult—afraid to hurt someone's feelings or let them down, afraid to be judged as lazy or unwilling to help, or afraid not to be faithfully serving God. My wife can't say no. She says she's afraid something fun might happen and she will miss out. Never mind that she is tired, empty, and exhausted—she'll volunteer for one more project.

In order to slow down your life, you need to understand why you have trouble saying no and then practice responding in the negative to some people or opportunities. Saying no will create some margin in your life for your heart to rest and reenergize. As Plato said, "It is better to do a little well, than a great deal badly."

Third, intentionally slow yourself down. If all you do is read books about how to be more efficient or listen to shows about how to manage your time to accomplish more, you are never going to slow down. You have to put your mind and energy into shifting to a slower gear.

Intentionally walk and talk slower (unless you live in West Texas, where my ranching buddies would be asleep if they moved or spoke any slower). I mean it. If you catch yourself walking speedily, intentionally slow your gait. Try a mosey or a saunter, even a slow strut. Here's a novel idea: let other people finish their sentences before you cut in. Chew your food before you swallow it. Turn off the radio to get some quiet in your car. Do only one thing at a time instead of multitasking. Read some of the postings on www.slowdownnow.org (the official website of the International Institute of Not Doing Much). Check out its manifesto:

Slow Manifesto
Do less, slowly

If you can slow down when all around you are speeding up, then you're one of us. Be proud that you are one of us and not one of them. For they are fast, and we are slow. There are those that would urge us to speed. We resist!

We shall not flag or fail. We shall slow down in the office, and on the roads. We shall slow down with growing confidence when all those around us are in a shrill state of hyperactivity

---

> (signifying nothing). We shall defend our state of calm, whatever the cost may be. We shall slow down in the fields and in the streets, we shall slow down in the hills, we shall never surrender!
>
> Why? Because if a thing is worth doing, it is worth doing slowly. Some are born to slowness—others have it thrust upon them. And still others know that lying in bed with a morning cup of tea is the supreme state for mankind.

Fourth, simplify. Life in today's America is amazingly complicated. We have stuff. We have stuff to organize our stuff. We have places to keep our stuff. The stuff is overtaking us.

I know people with psychological disorders who cannot get rid of stuff. These folks let it collect in their homes to the point that there is just enough walking space to get from room to room through the piles of stuff. The stuff by itself just gets in the way and is irritating to visitors.

But an even greater problem is that the stuff demands our energy and attention. Vacation homes are great stuff . . . but they take a lot of finances and energy to maintain. All our gadgets, gears, toys, and trinkets are great stuff . . . but they take up more than just space. They demand our resources—financial, mental, and emotional. As Richard Swenson points out, we are overloaded.

> If overload is sabotaging our equilibrium, simplicity can help. If we find ourselves overextended in our emotional, financial, and time commitments, simplicity is one of the best ways to reestablish margin.[8]

The solution is to simplify. Here are Greg and Shawn's top-ten favorite suggestions for simplifying:

1. Try to do only one thing at a time . . . stop multitasking.
2. Get rid of the time robbers in your life—television, surfing the Internet.
3. Make a list of the top four or five important things and focus on doing them well.
4. Get rid of clutter in your life.
5. Learn to say no.
6. Practice expressing gratitude for those who make your life easier.
7. Create a simplicity statement about what you want your simple life to look like.
8. Spend time alone.
9. Be present—fully engage the moment and place you are in.
10. Create morning and evening routines.

If our list is not exhaustive enough for you (we were trying to keep it simple), check out Joyce Meyer's *100 Ways to Simplify Your Life*[9] or Elaine St. James's *Simplify Your Life: 100 Ways to Slow Down and Enjoy the Things That Really Matter.*[10]

Simplifying means less stuff will demand your attention and energy. Simplifying allows you to slow down, as does resting, saying no, and getting intentional about your pace. You can slow down. Your life, your heart, and your marriage deserve it.

Slow down and feel the exhaustion ease, the heart open, and the connection begin.

Step 2: Recognize Your Value

The second step to move from an exhausted to a healthy heart is to recognize your value. While this is probably not as obvious a solution as slowing down, recognizing your value is just as significant in the process of relieving exhaustion and emptiness.

People who understand their value don't feel a pressure to perform to earn respect from others. People who understand their value have higher self-esteem and less depression and anxiety. People who understand their value respond better to stress and pressure. Thus, people who understand their value are less exhausted and empty . . . their hearts are healthier.

Unfortunately, the number of people who recognize and understand their value is pretty low. Our research indicates that "worthless" is the number one lie written on people's hearts.

A person who feels worthless has three options: (1) believe the lie and feel worthless, (2) work really hard to prove that the lie is false, or (3) understand the truth about where value and worth really come from.

For those who believe the lie, the path leads to anxiety, depression, and emptiness. For those who choose to work hard to disprove the lie, the path leads to exhaustion and perfectionism and a critical spirit. Both of the first two options lead to an empty, exhausted heart. Health comes only as we embrace the third path and understand our true value.

Why do so many people choose paths that lead to the destruction of their hearts? First, our culture has falsely defined value based on three parameters:

♡ Attractiveness—what you look like (are you pretty enough?)

♡ Accomplishments—what you do (is your job prestigious?)

♡ Accumulations—what you own (are your house and cars fancy enough?)

We silently judge ourselves in these three areas to see how we measure up. The comparisons never stop. Nor do they satisfy. Someone will always be more attractive, have a bigger salary, or have more "toys."

Forget keeping up with the Joneses; reality TV has us trying to keep up with all kinds of crazy celebrity families. On E! Network's *Keeping up with the Kardashians*, one of the kids just got a $100,000 Bentley. She actually "earned" the money for the car (accumulation) by using her beauty (attractiveness) to get a modeling job (accomplishments). By worldly standards, she has hit the value jackpot.

Yet there is no ultimate satisfaction in finding your value in these three areas. Attractiveness by our cultural standards fades with age, the thrill of accomplishments lasts only for a season, and our accumulations depreciate and wear out.

True value comes from somewhere else. The events surrounding the life and death of my (Shawn's) third child really showed us the truth about God's worth and value system. Christina went to the doctor halfway through her pregnancy for a checkup and ultrasound. The nurse practitioner informed Christina that there were some complications, possibly a cleft palate or other problems. Christina was referred to a specialist for a 3-D ultrasound.

At the specialist, we were informed that there were significant developmental problems. Our baby might make it to her delivery date, or she might spontaneously abort. Either way, the specialist informed us that she had no chance of survival after birth. Christina and I left the office, sat in our car for a good cry, then called all our friends and family who had been praying for us. With each call, we went over what the doctor had told us along with the long list of developmental problems.

Finally, we told our then seven-year-old daughter, Taylor. We went through the same story and list with Taylor, but she responded differently. Taylor said, "Okay, you've told me what all is wrong with my sister. Now tell me what is good about her. There must be something." She was right. We did have a little girl growing inside of Christina with a heart that was beating strong. We immediately gave her a name, Avery. We prayed for her, talked to her, and celebrated the fact that she was ours.

The next four months of the pregnancy were difficult as we anticipated the birth process, but we continued to love Avery any way we could think of. When the day finally came, we headed to the hospital. The doctors told us that the best-case scenario would be for us to get a couple of hours with Avery after delivery, because her lungs could not sustain her life any longer than that.

I will never forget watching Avery kicking Christina's stomach from inside the womb. Unfortunately, the delivery was just too traumatic for fragile Avery. The doctor let me "catch" her as she came out, but she was not breathing. Her heart was no longer beating. Finally, I held my little girl while simultaneously her spirit was headed somewhere else to be held.

I would have given anything to see her smile, or move, or cough, or even breathe. At that moment she was the most precious, valuable thing in the whole world to me. She was not attractive by earthly standards (covered in birth fluid and squished from the delivery), she had not accomplished anything (Christina had done all the work to even get her out into the room), and she had accumulated nothing (naked with no possessions). And yet Avery was the most valuable thing in the world to us. Because she was ours.

You and I are the same way. We are valuable because the Creator of the universe knit us together in our mothers' wombs. We are valuable because we are His. Our value comes from the fact that we belong to God—He made us, redeemed us, and loves us. End of story.

We might *expect* our culture to give us a false definition of value, but a second problem arises from the message we sometimes get from the Christian community. The world we live in is a selfish place with people constantly clamoring that life is all about them. To counter this, the Christian community has swung the pendulum to the other extreme. Instead if "it's all about me," we counter with "it's not about me."

The first sentence of Rick Warren's wildly successful book *The Purpose Driven Life* reads, "It's not about you."[11] Max Lucado evidently liked Warren's idea so much that he followed with an entire book called *It's Not About Me*.[12] While I understand their well-intentioned efforts to keep us from believing that life is all about us, I disagree with the totality of the statement. I believe that life is at least partially about us.

The danger in these statements is that if we continue to tell Christians that it is not about them, we imply that they have no value—that they really are worthless. And this is just not true. You do have value, and it is partially (not all, but at least some) about you.

First, God sent His Son to die on a cross for the forgiveness of *your* sins. I have heard many preachers say He would have done that even if you were the only person on earth. Doesn't that seem like it is about you?

Second, Jesus tells an interesting parable about a shepherd

with a hundred sheep (see Luke 15:4–7). In the story, one of them gets away, and the shepherd leaves the ninety-nine behind to go find that straggler. I (Shawn) am somewhat ashamed to say that I have been around sheep. If you ever got ninety-nine of your sheep in one place, you would not leave to look for the other one. Because the second you turn your back on the big group, they will scatter, and you will be left rounding them all up again. But the Bible's shepherd goes after that one no matter what happens to the group. In that moment, it is about that one.

You are that one. It is about you. The Bible is the story of God's love and pursuit of you, His desire to reconcile you to a relationship with Him, and His coming back for you. It is about you—not all about you, not you more than anyone else, but some about you.

If you were to plot it on a line, it would look something like this:

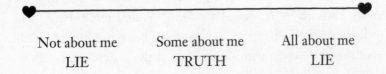

Not about me   Some about me   All about me
LIE   TRUTH   LIE

Let's stop telling Christians it's not about them, thus devaluing who God created us to be. God bless Max Lucado (a good ol' West Texas boy). His next book was called *Cure for the Common Life* and was all about finding your unique value from God and using it to make a difference in the lives of others to ultimately glorify God.[13] Yes, you are valuable because God made you, and He don't make no junk.

Here are a couple of practical applications to help you see the connection between your value and your exhausted heart.

First, recognizing the source of your value and worth lets you exhale and rest. You cannot earn any more value than what you already have. Your value does not come from what you do—it comes from who you are. The son of a king is a prince, not because he killed a dragon but because his dad is already royalty. It works the same for you—your Father is the Creator of the universe, therefore you are valuable.

Second, get alone with God and ask Him what makes you *uniquely* valuable to Him. You are valuable, worthy, and accepted because you are His, but that is also true of everyone else in the world. You are uniquely valuable because you were created in His image and He deposited a specific attribute of Himself in you. Ask Him what it is. What unique gifting do you have?

Over the years, we have heard from countless people who have asked God this question. Here is a sampling of His responses to them (all unique and specific):

♡ You are a seer with the ability to read people's hearts.

♡ You are a safe place of refuge.

♡ You are a bold truthteller.

♡ You are a joy giver to those around you.

♡ You are empathetic with the ability to feel the pain of others.

♡ You have a passionate, contagious faith.

♡ You have exceptional analytical and clear-thinking abilities.

♡ You uniquely see and understand the long-term perspective.

♡ You are an amazing encourager.

♡ You unconditionally accept people.

♡ You are a generous giver who shares his blessings with others.

♡ You are gifted with the ability to inspire others through music and praise.

♡ You perfectly balance logic and compassion.

Your life does not need to be measured by a list of accomplishments. God longs for you to know that you are valuable because you are His. He also desires for you to understand what makes you uniquely special and valuable to Him. You can rest in these truths. You can find healing for the exhausted empty heart inside you. You can bless others with the knowledge that you are uniquely gifted and talented to make a difference in their lives.

Step 3: Get Whole and Full

Recognizing the true source of your value sets you up for success in the last step of healing the exhausted heart: getting whole and full.

We tend to take care of things that we consider valuable—wedding ring, new car, golf clubs, the kids (hopefully). Nothing in our lives needs more taking care of these days than ourselves. Neglecting ourselves has left us in quite a predicament. As Swenson put it: "Overworked and overwhelmed victims occupy our no-margin world."[14]

Christina and I (Shawn) found ourselves in this predicament a few years back. We moved from Texas to Branson, Missouri—where all the old country-and-western singers go to live out their last days—to help start the Marriage Intensive program at the Smalley Relationship Center.

Because I am a good steward of the resources the Lord has entrusted to us (or, as Christina would say, because I'm cheap), I thought it would be a good idea to get a travel trailer and live in a campground until we found a good home to purchase. Christina and the kids were up to the adventure, but none of us knew it would last two months. I found a nice campground with shaded trees and a pool (about the size of a really big bathtub). And so we began our new life in Missouri.

I was working in a new place, meeting new people, and learning new things. Christina was in the trailer, twelve hundred miles from home, taking care of a six-year-old and a three-year-old. We were in a city where she knew no one, and the average age of the other occupants of the campground was about seventy. It didn't take long for the early signs of depression and anger to start showing up in Christina.

I soon wondered if we had moved to Branson to *give* marriage counseling or to *get* it, because our marriage was hurting. Christina kept getting more and more empty and exhausted. One day, I came home (to the trailer) from work and had this interchange with Christina.

Christi: I am sick of this trailer.

Shawn: You have to get outside more.

Christi: We don't know anyone. There is nowhere to go.

Shawn: Go to the pool.

Christi: If I see one more seventy-five-year-old man in a Speedo bathing suit, I am going to kill him. Then I am going to hook this trailer up and head back home to Texas.

She was worn out with nothing left to give. She was out of energy. Her heart was empty. At that point, Christina was no different from almost all the people who come to marriage intensive sessions—she was empty and exhausted.

The solution to this exhaustion epidemic is simple: take care of yourself to get back to whole and full.

As a group, we evangelical Christians in North America do not do a good job of taking care of ourselves. This is true for a couple of reasons.

First, we have been taught that it is selfish to care for ourselves. Church signs proclaim: JOY with J = Jesus first, O = others second, Y = yourself last. Church camps give out the "I'm Third" award to campers who give the most of themselves. A friend recently saw a kid wearing a T-shirt that read "I'm so third that I'm fourth." These messages make great signs, slogans, and T-shirts, but they take quite a toll on us if we try to live them out.

Constantly putting yourself third (or last behind everyone else) leaves you empty and exhausted. This can't really be God's formula, can it? A bunch of empty, exhausted people have nothing to give and no way to serve.

Actually, God lays out His formula in the Great Commandment. "'Love the Lord your God with all your heart and with all your soul and with all your mind and with all your strength.' The second is this: 'Love your neighbor as yourself'" (Mark 12:30–31). The "as yourself" part is critical. You cannot just ignore that. It does not say love your neighbor *before* yourself. You must be taking care of yourself so that you have something to give to your neighbor (or spouse).

It is not selfish to take care of yourself. Jesus modeled self-care—often withdrawing to the wilderness to be alone, sending crowds of people away to be with His friends, going to social events when He could have been "working," sleeping while everyone else was panicking, and once even hiding from His disciples. Jesus was not selfish; He was simply doing what He needed to do to prevent exhaustion and emptiness.

Many pastors I know would benefit from His example. Actually, all of us would benefit from recognizing that taking care of ourselves is not selfish. It may be the best thing you could possibly do for your family, because then they receive the blessing of a whole, full you.

Obviously, the goal of this taking care of yourself in a healthy way is so that you can have something to give to the people around you. Thus, the formula has you taking care of yourself, getting full, sharing that with the people you are serving and loving in relationship, getting low or empty, then starting back over with self-care.

A second reason we may not take good care of ourselves is that we believe it is someone else's job to do that. Movies love to romanticize the idea that you are half full and can somehow find the one person in the universe who can complete you. Many a codependent marriage has tried to succeed on the premise that two people can somehow come together to make a whole. If your spouse is not taking care of you, you just coerce, guilt, or manipulate him or her into doing a better job.

Unfortunately, it's just not that simple. No one else can complete you. Only you and God working together can make you whole, full, and healthy. God's view of marriage is not that a half + a half = a whole. His view is that a whole + a whole = something really spectacular. You cannot delegate this job—you are responsible for taking care of yourself.

A third reason we do not take good care of ourselves is that we don't know how. There is a shortage of good role models out there. On the one hand, we see people who try to fill the emptiness with temporary substitutes (like work, alcohol, other people, money, possessions, or pleasure). These substitutes offer brief relief but no long-term satisfaction. They leave people feeling more empty, which forces them to seek more of the same, and right there you have the makings of a good addiction cycle.

On the other hand, you have the people who avoid the substitutes but also deny themselves. They serve themselves to death. Christina watched her mom serve, clean, host, mentor, tutor, intercede . . . always to the exclusion of herself. She ended up empty and exhausted, praying for the strength to wake up the next day and do it all over again. Neither of these extremes produces good role models.

In God's plan, people should take care of themselves, receive from Him, get their hearts full and whole, and then overflow that fullness onto the people around them.

Paul prayed, "May the God of hope fill you with all joy and peace as you trust in him, so that you may overflow with hope by the power of the Holy Spirit" (Romans 15:13). In similar fashion, Jesus shared with others so that His joy would be in them and that their joy would be complete. Then they could love others as He loved them (see John 15:11–12). We are commanded to comfort others with the comfort we ourselves have received from God (see 2 Corinthians 1:4). And as we saw earlier, we can only love others because God first loved us (see 1 John 4:19).

In each of these verses, the pattern is the same: we must stop to receive from the Lord before we can bless others. That's a good formula: God first, us next to receive, others third to pass it along to. That's good self-care.

The work of self-care focuses on four areas. These areas are taken right from the Great Commandment: it is with all our *hearts, souls, minds, and strength* that we are to love God, others, and ourselves.

Think and pray through the following self-test. On a scale of

0 (not at all) to 25 (totally), rate how full you are in each area. Listed are some actions to prompt your thinking as you score yourself. How full are you . . .

_____ Emotionally (heart)? Much of this book is about caring for your heart. You can get full emotionally by understanding and identifying your feelings and expressing them appropriately, sharing in healthy edifying relationships, journaling, grieving losses, celebrating successes, playing, laughing, and allowing yourself to be deeply touched.

_____ Spiritually (soul)? You can get full spiritually through connection with God, worship, Bible study, prayer time, listening to God, and small-group fellowship.

_____ Mentally (mind)? You can get full mentally through positive thoughts, sense of value and worth, growing intellectually, reading, exchanging ideas with others, and avoiding feeding your mind unhealthy images.

_____ Physically (strength)? You can get full physically through eating healthy food, getting cardiovascular exercise, sleeping, drinking water, lifting weights, experiencing adventure, stretching.

Add up your scores in the four areas and get a total (take a point off your mental score if you need to use a calculator). How did you do? Because there were 100 total points, your score is a rough indicator of how full you are. This is how much energy you have to share with others.

With most married couples, the first 50 to 75 percent of their energy goes into work and the children. If that were true for you, would you have anything left for your spouse? Which areas could you put a little more effort into to stay whole and full?

To combat the exhaustion epidemic, we must all try to do things to keep our fullness scores on the rise. There is one great role model. The only thing we know about Jesus from the age of about thirteen to thirty years old as He prepared for the ministry that would change the world is summed up in Luke 2:52—"Jesus grew in wisdom and stature, and in favor with God and men."

In that verse, we are told that Jesus grew in four areas. You guessed it: wisdom (mentally), stature (physically), favor with God (spiritually), and favor with men (emotionally). Throughout His three-year ministry, Jesus continued to revisit and recharge in each of these areas.

That's our challenge—to take care of ourselves in these four areas so that we stay full of the energy and resources necessary to avoid exhaustion and to bless those around us.

I have had the privilege of being around a few people who were committed to good self-care. They are the exact opposite of selfish. They are without a doubt the most loving, serving, giving people I know. Keep in mind that to the extent that you are whole and full, you are free to love fully and unconditionally.

THE EXHAUSTED HEART
IN MARRIAGE

Mennonite author Doris Longacre observed:

Much of the fatigue in the Western world takes place in the name of making money, even though the pantry's already stocked. After all, by burning a little more gas and working one more evening a week, it is possible to chase down one more account, open another store, or farm another field. But it may not be possible to love a spouse, children, and the friendless poor at the same time.[15]

All of our ceaseless striving is costing us in one key area: our relationships.

Exhausted people have nothing to share with each other at the end of the day (when most of us get our first real alone time with our spouses). By that time, hearts are depleted and energy is zapped. We try to hold out for a date night or a weekend, but even then we often have little to give to the person who means the most to us.

In conflict situations, the exhausted heart does even more damage. Being tired magnifies into full-blown battles what might at other times be just minor annoyances. Empty, exhausted people rarely come up with loving things to say in these tense interchanges.

On the other hand, there are people who slow down and simplify, recognize their value, and take the time to get whole and full. These people open their hearts and overflow with love into their spouses. Conflict is rare and quickly resolved if encountered. Demands and expectations of others are minimal. Fun and laughter come easily. Wholehearted marriage in this scenario is amazing.

Your marriage is worth it . . . attend to that exhausted heart.

LOOKING AHEAD

The final three chapters of *The Wholehearted Marriage* fall into the section on unleashing the heart. In chapters 1 to 2 we got an understanding of the heart and its importance. In chapters 3 to 5 we explored how your heart gets taken out and what you can do to reengage it in life and marriage. In chapters 6 to 8 we want to address how to engage your spouse's heart so that together you can experience a wholehearted marriage.

PART THREE
Unleashing the Heart

Chapter 6
Caring for Your Mate's Heart

In the same way, you husbands must give honor to your wives. Treat your wife with understanding as you live together.

—1 Peter 3:7 NLT

Carry each other's burdens, and in this way you will fulfill the law of Christ.

—Galatians 6:2

I DON'T CARE what you know until I know that you care." It's a John Maxwell quote you may have heard before. A few years back that thought took on a different significance for me.

One morning, I (Shawn) walked into my bathroom and found those words written with dry-erase marker on my mirror. Quotes just seem to mean more when they are etched on the place usually reserved for my bed-head reflection. Christina was sending me a clear message. Specifically, it was tied to our fight the night before, but more generally it was a clear indictment of how I tended to interact with her.

My goal in our interactions centered on analyzing problems and giving solutions. I was eager to fix, offering wise counsel and advice. The problem was that all of that came from my head. Christina has never been interested in a relationship with just my head. She wanted my heart. She was not impressed by how smart I was or how good a solution I could come up with; she just wanted me to care about her and what she was feeling. Before I gave my opinions, she wanted me to show some compassion.

I am evidently not alone in this particular problem. Perhaps men more stereotypically fall into this pattern of communication, but many women suffer the same affliction. We want to help each other, and providing information and solutions seems like the logical way to do that. However, our marriages need more than fixing. They need honest, genuine, caring connection. Two hearts open to each other so that love and compassion can flow. Not two heads butting up against each other trying to win a power struggle or hammer out a compromise.

We have often minimized the power of caring in a relationship. Simply caring. I guess we assume caring is so easy. "Of course, we care . . . why else would we still be here? Let's skip to something meaty, like offering amazing insight or impressive solutions. Are you sure caring is essential?"

Christina seems to think so, as do most of the people we counsel. Even more important, God believes in this caring thing. How many times have you prayed for Him to fix all your problems? You know, turn all the lights green so I can get to work on time, open up a parking space next to the grocery store, strike my mean boss down with some kind of illness. We all ask God to fix things and solve our problems, and sometimes He does. But not usually.

The lights turn red, someone cuts in from the wrong direction to claim your parking space, and your boss stays healthy while you get a headache. God does not always "fix," but He does always "care." He cares, He loves, He empathizes, He shows compassion, and He is always there. God cares, and it makes a difference.

Knowing that your heart, your feelings, and your situation matter to the Creator of the universe does make you feel better. God cares about you. And God is a great model when it comes to "fixing." He tends to care first and offer solutions later (and only when necessary).

Caring for your spouse's heart is critical for a successful marriage. You are married to a person with an amazingly valuable and incredibly vulnerable heart. When you two said *I do*, you pledged to care for each other. In sickness and in health 'till death do you part, you agreed to care for your spouse. Not just in terms of financial provision and the meeting of sexual needs, but in ways deeper and more significant.

The heart is the essence of your spouse, the valuable center of who he or she is. When your mate opens and grants you access, you get the most wonderful opportunity in the world—the chance to care for the most sacred part of your spouse.

It's true that your mate could choose to shut down and wall you out of access to his or her heart. But as we have shown, if a spouse takes good care of himself or herself and feels safe with you, then the heart will open. You will be granted access. In that moment, your job description is simple: *care*.

But what does that mean? Glad you asked.

Caring is a process that includes communicating to understand, allowing compassion to flow, and expressing care through empathy and validation.

COMMUNICATE TO UNDERSTAND

No marriage book worth its salt could fail to address the topic of communication. Communication, or the lack of it, is widely accepted as one of the main reasons for marital strife. But before you're tempted to skip over this section with a "been there, done that" attitude, we want to warn you that this will be different.

Most teaching about communication is designed to help us in head-to-head situations. This book is all about helping you get heart to heart. Therefore, the goal of this communication section is to give you the keys to unlock your spouse's heart.

Step 1—Talk about Talking

Picture the following scenario:

Christina has planned a party for some of our closest friends. I recognize that the lawn has been neglected and the grass is high enough to lose a small child in. I head out for some mowing, thankful that I don't have to do any of the indoor cleanup and party preparation. Unlike Greg, I love mowing the lawn—strips of freshly cut grass display the tangible results of my labor (unlike my marriage counseling some days).

Halfway through mowing the front yard, I notice some smoke coming out of the lawnmower. A couple of laps later, the mower has stopped. My lawn looks like the equivalent of a bad Mohawk, short on the sides and very long in the middle.

At the same moment, Christina is inside, cleaning the kitchen, when she notices water coming out of the bottom of the dishwasher. She turns it off and begins to think about how much additional time it will take to get ready for the party without the dishwasher to aid her. Christina plops down at the table and picks up the phone to call her friend.

Christi: You are not going to believe what just happened.

Tammy: What?

Christi: I was getting ready for the party, when the dishwasher broke.

Tammy: Oh, my goodness. I am so sorry. And you have all those people coming over for the party. You must feel awful.

I'm still in the front yard with the broken lawn mower, so I sit down on the steps and pick up my cell phone.

Shawn: You are not going to believe what just happened.

Dave: What?

Shawn: I was in the middle of mowing for this party Christina is having, when the lawnmower broke.

Dave: What happened with the mower? Was there smoke or did it run out of gas? Take the air filter off, clean it up, and screw it back on. Check the oil. Then give it another try.

Did you catch the difference? Look at the last response from Christina's friend as compared to how my friend responded. What if those responses got reversed? What would happen if I called Dave to tell him about my broken lawnmower and he responded, "Oh, I am so sorry. With the party coming up, I bet you are going to be embarrassed. How does that make your heart feel?" I would hang up on him and call Doug. I would tell Doug that I needed help getting my lawnmower fixed—and that something was wrong with Dave.

In similar fashion, what would happen if Christina's friend had responded, "Shoot, Christi, just turn off the breaker to the dishwasher, pull that thing straight out, grab a pipe wrench, and turn the hot water hose three-quarter turn clockwise?" Christina would say, "What do you think I have a husband for? I was just looking for a little empathy."

This scenario illustrates that men and women have different reasons for communicating. Sometimes we talk to solve problems and fix stuff. Guys are particularly wired for this kind of communication. Other times we talk to connect and care about each other, but women are usually better suited for this kind of communication.

• Problems arise when one member of the conversation wants to connect but the other member is trying to fix. Generally speaking, *fixing* is head-level communication whereas *connecting* is heart-level communication. We are all capable of both kinds of communication. Success occurs when we are on the same page regarding the goal of the conversation.

The first step in communicating to understand is being willing to *talk about talking*. Before you even start a conversation, try the following:

1. Make sure you agree that this is a good time to talk. When you call a friend on the phone, you often begin with "Is this a good time to talk?" Your spouse deserves this same courtesy. Make sure your spouse is ready to begin a conversation. A good

indication may be if he or she is willing to at least mute the TV.

2. Agree on the goal. Do you want to connect or do you want to fix something? Contrary to what some people will tell you, men don't always want to fix and women don't always want to connect. In the scenario I described above, Christina came out on the front porch to tell me about the dishwasher. I responded like a counselor (or one of her friends), "Oh, baby, I am so sorry. That is a bummer." She said, "I don't need empathy, you goofball, I need you to get in here and fix the dishwasher." (This is why women sometimes get labeled "hard to figure out.")

3. Check in during the conversation. Stop at appropriate intervals in the dialogue to make sure you are both still on the same page. Ask questions like, "Am I understanding you right?" "Is that what you are saying?" or "Are we meeting the goal we established for this conversation?" In the middle of a conversation, particularly a heated discussion, it is easy to lose track of what you are trying to accomplish. Be willing to remind each other, "Remember, I just need you to try to understand what I am saying, not give me solutions."

Talking about talking will save you lots of headaches and misunderstandings in your communication. On the other hand, not setting up the rules of a conversation and not checking in to stay on track leads to frustration and disconnection.

Recently Christina came to me while I was watching television. She started in about how difficult the morning had been trying to get the kids out of bed, dressed, fed, presentable for public display, packed up, and headed to school on time. I kept one eye on ESPN (in my defense, it was the fourth quarter) and half listened to her story.

As soon as she paused to take a breath, I gave her a brilliant analysis and solution. "You should set the kids' clothes out the night before, have each of them set an alarm clock, develop a reward system for getting up and ready independently . . ." I was on a roll and this stuff was good (possibly a parenting book in the making without Greg).

Somewhere midway through my lecture, I realized Christina was not paying attention. I tried to get her attention by talking louder and reminding her that she was the one who came to me with the issue. She looked me right in the eye and said, "Do you think I am an idiot? I know how to get the kids to school in the morning. I just wanted to connect with you for a few minutes by telling you about my day!" I had pushed her "not good enough" button.

In that brief yet painful interchange we violated all three of the "talk about talking" steps. Christina did not ask me if it was a good time to talk or at least wait for a commercial. I did not ask her what she needed from me: connection or solutions. In this case, Christina just wanted to connect with me. We did not pause in the middle to see why we were getting off track. And the result was hurt feelings and confusion.

It pays to talk about your communication.

Step 2—Avoid the Pitfalls

The second step in communicating to understand is to avoid pitfalls in your talks. If you both have agreed that the goal is to connect and understand each other, you can begin your dialogue. However, simply agreeing on a common goal will not guarantee success. You need to avoid the pitfalls that prevent most couples from communicating on a heart level.

- ♡ Pitfall 1: trying to figure out who is right or wrong. My wife used to end arguments by saying in a totally sarcastic voice, "As always, O Great and Wise Counselor, you are 100 percent right and I am 100 percent wrong." Her tactic worked. I would shut up and ask myself, *Do I really want to be right more than I want to care about her?* Many of us fall into the trap of trying to prove our point or win the argument. Remember, heart-level communication is about understanding, not winning.

- ♡ Pitfall 2: trying to figure out who is to blame or at fault. We also love to assign responsibility. From an early age, we learn to blame others. "You made me feel this way when you (fill in the blank)." Blaming each other robs us of getting a chance to simply care.

- ♡ Pitfall 3: trying to figure out what was said or what really happened. A typical interaction might look like this:

Husband:	What's wrong?
Wife:	I can't believe you said *that* earlier.
Husband:	I did not say *that* earlier.
Wife:	You certainly did say *that*.
Husband:	Well, I did not say it like *that*.
Wife:	I am the one who heard you say it.

195

Husband: Well, I should know how I said it
since I am the one who said it.

Pointless interaction, but fairly typical. We argue about what was said and how it was said. And yet those things are irrelevant to getting understanding. Even if you do figure out the exact words that were spoken, research indicates that you would have only about 8 percent of the meaning of the message (the other 92 percent of the meaning is communicated in the tone, facial expression, and posture).

If you are like most of the couples we work with, you will fall into at least one of these pits about 90 percent of the time in your conflicts. Figuring out who is right or wrong is a waste of time because you and your spouse are teammates. You are trying to connect with each other, not win some contest. Figuring out who is to blame is a waste of time because you don't really want someone to be responsible for your well-being; you just want him or her to care about you. And figuring out what was really said is a waste of time because it is much more important to find out what was heard and how it impacted the listener.

There is a better way. Seek to understand and connect while avoiding the pitfalls.

Step 3—Extinguish the Relational Germs

The third step in communicating to understand is to go after those "germs" that can sicken a marriage. While the pitfalls listed above are directions your conversations need to avoid; relational germs are self-protective coping behaviors or reactions that show up in our relationships. Based on the extensive research of John Gottman at the University of Washington,[1] these four relational germs (reactions to protect ourselves) emerged as predictors of doom to a relationship:

- ♡ Germ 1: criticism—attacking your spouse's personality or character. "You always . . . ," "You never . . . ," "Why are you so . . . ?"
- ♡ Germ 2: contempt—disrespecting the essence of who your spouse is. "You are a failure."
- ♡ Germ 3: defensiveness—protecting yourself and your point without listening to your spouse. "Yes, but . . . ," "It's not my fault," "That's not true."
- ♡ Germ 4: stonewalling—withdrawing and shutting down to avoid. "I am out of here."

These germs are deadly because they become pervasive coping mechanisms that close down our hearts and make it unsafe for those around us. With closed hearts, there is no room to care. Communication becomes toxic, connection disappears, and understanding is never attained.

Think back to your last conflict with your spouse. Did either of you use any of these germs as your fight-or-flight mechanism? They must be extinguished at all costs, replaced with healthier ways of interacting.

Step 4—Seek to Understand

The richest man to ever live, King Solomon, said, "Though it costs all you have, get understanding" (Proverbs 4:7). Earlier in the same book, he recommended "applying your heart to understanding" (Proverbs 2:2). Here is this amazingly rich and incredibly wise man telling us to seek understanding.

If we desire a wholehearted marriage, we must apply our hearts to understanding—particularly the understanding of our spouses' feelings. When tensions rise and tempers flare, seek to understand your spouse's heart. When tears flow and hurt is evident, seek to understand your spouse's heart. When wounds are exposed and buttons are triggered, seek to understand your spouse's heart.

How important is understanding? The apostle Peter offers the following guidance in the New Testament: "Husbands, in the same way be considerate [understanding] as you live with your wives . . . so that nothing will hinder your prayers" (1 Peter 3:7). It doesn't take a seminary education to get the gist of this verse. For us husbands, being caring in our interactions with our wives is so significant that a failure to understand them could lead to a disconnect in our communication with God. That's a big deal.

Experts tell us that up to 80 percent of conflicts are simply the result of misunderstanding.[2] In a study of more than fifty thousand couples, communicating to understand was found to be the number one indicator of marital happiness.[3]

There is a simple phrase that could change your marriage forever. Get ready for it. Don't skip ahead. The anticipation is building. Okay, here it is . . .

"HELP ME UNDERSTAND"

Not too flashy as you read it in a book, but man, is it powerful. Wife is crying; you respond, "Help me understand." Husband is angry; you respond, "Help me understand." Your child is shutting down; you respond, "Help me understand." It's an amazing sentence.

"Help me" communicates humility and a desire for something different. It's a posture shift away from trying to win or blame to trying to connect and care. It puts the other person at ease and even in a position of giving instruction.

If "Help me understand" is not your typical response in a difficult interaction, your spouse may be surprised at your first use of it. Don't give up. Keep communicating your desire to understand. When your spouse feels your genuine desire to care and connect, his or her heart will feel safer and hearts will begin to open up.

ALLOW COMPASSION TO FLOW

Communicating to understand is powerful because it changes the posture of the heart—your heart and the heart of the person you are interacting with. Your heart opens with curiosity and care. The other person's heart opens in the presence of your safe concern for his or her feelings. Now with two hearts open, you are free to connect.

Once your heart is touched, compassion becomes the motivating force for caring. Just as passion provides the energy to accomplish a task or a goal, compassion provides the motivation for expressing care to your spouse. The art of caring is allowing the compassion that you are feeling to flow freely from your open heart to your spouse.

Compassion is incredibly important in a marriage. After much study and after having written many books on love and anger and relationships, Dr. Steven Stosny concluded:

Compassion is the most important emotion in marriage and intimate relationships, contributing far more to happiness than love does. Relationships can be happy with low levels of love and high levels of compassion, but not the other way around.[4]

Compassion is the feeling that your spouse's heart really matters. It says that whatever is going on in there—the fears, wounds, hurts, desires, passions—it is all important. Your mate's heart, like yours, is amazingly valuable and vulnerable. You can compassionately communicate that you value his or her heart in a number of ways—through words, a certain look, a touch, or actions. Whatever the manifestation, compassion always communicates care and understanding.

Our compassion is simply a reflection of the compassion we receive from the God in whose image we were created. "The LORD is gracious and righteous; our God is full of compassion" (Psalm 116:5). Jesus provides us the ultimate example of this: "When he saw the crowds, he had compassion on them, because they were harassed and helpless, like sheep without a shepherd" (Matthew 9:36). Frequently, the miracles He performed to heal people were motivated by compassion.

But that's God, not you, right? It's one thing to read about it in the Bible. It becomes increasingly more difficult when you are asked to show compassion to someone who has hurt you. Just like it is tough to say "Help me understand" when the person across from you is yelling at you, it is often very hard to show compassion when you are wounded by your spouse.

Yet again we have a great illustration from Scripture. In the story of the prodigal son, the father (who gave the boy a great home and a sizable inheritance, only to be abandoned) had every right to be angry, hurt, and bitter. But that is not how the story goes. "But while he was still a long way off, his father saw him and was filled with compassion for him; he ran to his son, threw his arms around him and kissed him" (Luke 15:20).

There's that word again—compassion. The father's heart, filled with compassion, motivated him to care and embrace and forgive.

And so it can be with you. You have the opportunity to show compassion to your spouse. Opening your heart, motivated to care, willing to embrace the valuable and vulnerable part of who he or she is. We have been called to live and love this way: "Therefore, as God's chosen people, holy and dearly loved, clothe yourselves with compassion, kindness, humility, gentleness and patience" (Colossians 3:12).

There are some practical steps that will allow you to put on that compassion.

Step 1: Open the Eyes of Your Heart

Paul prayed in Ephesians 1:18 that "the eyes of your heart may be enlightened in order that you may know." When we open our hearts to others we have the ability to see in a totally different way.

With the eyes of your heart you can see your toddler as tired or hungry, not as a brat lying in a crying heap pitching a fit on the floor. With the eyes of your heart you can see a friend who is hurting from a broken relationship, not as the pessimistic woman across from you who is always complaining. With the eyes of your heart you can see a husband who is exhausted from a hard day instead of the guy sitting in front of the television vegging out.

Ask God to open the eyes of your heart toward your mate.

Step 2: Treat Your Spouse's Heart As Valuable and Vulnerable

Think of your most prized possession. Maybe your wedding ring, your golf clubs, or your new car. Now think of the lengths you go to in an effort to take care of that prized possession. You have insurance on it, you know where it is at all times, you clean it.

Now consider how valuable your spouse's heart is.

Not only is it valuable, it is also incredibly vulnerable. In counseling we sometimes have a person hold a teddy bear to represent his or her spouse's heart. Even grown men will gently hold a teddy bear (in the confidential privacy of a counseling setting where no other man will ever know). We try to get these guys used to treating something with tenderness.

Compassion flows when you recognize that your spouse is granting you access to a very valuable, vulnerable place. In the presence of your spouse's heart, you must act with care and gentleness. You must tread lightly. Granted access to this special place, you should hold your spouse's heart in the way you would hold a newborn baby.

Too many times we have witnessed a man finally open his heart, only to have his wife respond with "It's about time," or "Well, you really need to do some cleaning up in here," or "Let me tell you what you should do next." She drops the "baby," and he closes back up. Men are often at least as bad. A precious wife opens her heart in genuine vulnerability, only to hear "Stop crying," "Don't let that bother you so much," or "It's not my fault." He tears up the teddy bear, and she closes back up.

When granted access to your spouse's heart, never lose sight of how valuable and vulnerable it truly is. Be gentle with it.

Step 3: Care Without Blaming

Trying to assign responsibility gets in the way of compassion. It is hard to open and really care when our heads are battling it out over who is to blame.

Continually blaming someone and trying to get that person to take responsibility for the problem robs you both of the opportunity to simply care. Rather than saying, "You make me feel . . . ," which assigns blame, try saying, "I was feeling . . . ," which gives your spouse a chance to show some compassion.

Do your heart and your marriage a favor: set aside the need to assign blame and work on simply caring.

These three steps will clear the way for a compassionate connection for you and your spouse.

EXPRESS EMPATHY AND VALIDATION FOR YOUR MATE'S HEART

Seeking to understand opens the door to your spouse's heart and begins the caring process. Compassion provides the internal motivation to care. The tools that express your care in a tangible way are empathy and validation.

Empathy says, "I feel what you are feeling, and I want to share in your joy (or pain)." Validation says, "What you are feeling matters to me and you matter to me." Empathy expresses connection on an emotional level. Validation expresses connection on a psychological level. Both empathy and validation are essential to the caring process.

When Jesus lived on earth, he personally felt anger, sadness, disappointment, joy, and pain. He also shared in the emotional experiences of those closest to Him. We can learn a great deal about empathy from the way Jesus responded when Lazarus died.

> When Jesus saw [Mary] weeping, and the Jews who had come along with her also weeping, he was deeply moved in spirit and troubled.
> "Where have you laid him?" he asked.
> "Come and see, Lord," they replied.
> Jesus wept.
> Then the Jews said, "See how he loved him!" (John 11:33–36)

First, allow your open heart to be impacted. Jesus was "deeply moved in spirit." Second, allow your heart to feel right along with what others are feeling. Jesus joined them in weeping. Third, allow your empathy to be motivated by compassion. Jesus' weeping illustrated His compassion. Others noticed, saying "See how he loved him!"

Fourth, allow empathy to be enough. You may feel pressure to make others' feelings go away, but follow Jesus' example and just sit with them in their emotions. It is worth noting that Jesus did eventually raise Lazarus from the dead. But even knowing He was going to do that, Jesus took the time to first empathize with His friends.

Sometimes just sitting with people in their emotions is the most difficult thing in the world to do. We want to offer solutions or make them snap out of it. Romans 12:15 offers some good advice: "Rejoice with those who rejoice; mourn with those who mourn." Meet them where they are and stay there with them.

Most of us don't like that formula. We would rather it said, "Find people who are mourning and try to get them to rejoice." Unfortunately, that is not biblical and not usually helpful. There may come a time when the best thing to do is cheer people up, but that will always follow a period of sitting in their pain with them.

The Bible describes the union of a man and a woman in marriage as "they will become one flesh" (Genesis 2:24). An obvious manifestation of this would be the ability to feel what the other is feeling.

When my wife is hurting, she does not want to hear me say, "Snap out of it." She does not want me to compare her situation to someone less fortunate so that she will feel guilty. She does not want me to ignore her and pretend nothing is going on. My wife wants me to care about what is happening in her heart.

Compassion for her says, "I feel for you." Empathy for her takes the next step and says, "I feel *with* you."

She wants me to take a moment to put myself in her shoes, see things from her perspective, and attempt to experience her emotional world. When I do this, we have some of the most amazing, heartfelt connections. She feels understood and cared for—like her heart really matters to me.

We guys may have to work a little harder at empathy because it does not seem to come naturally. Some researchers agree with one author that "the female brain is predominantly hard-wired for empathy while the male brain is predominantly hard-wired for understanding and building systems."[5] There's even a test you can take online to determine your empathy quotient.[6]

Hard-wired or not, women do get more practice with empathy than men. Most men in our culture make a living based on how well they can understand and solve problems. Empathy is not a valued skill on most job sites. You won't usually hear a man say, "You seem a little sad today, Phil. After we finish pouring this concrete and welding those columns, let's sit down so I can join you in your suffering."

As foolish as he would be to say something like that at work, most men have a wife at home longing to hear words like those. Marriages thrive when empathy is practiced often. So, ladies, give him some coaching and give him a chance.

Like empathy, validation is a critical way to express the connection between your heart and your spouse's heart. Sometimes the heart just does not make sense. How many times have you heard someone say, "I just don't know why I am letting this bother me"? Sometimes buttons get triggered inadvertently. Without meaning to or without even being aware of it, your spouse may begin feeling one of those messages from the past: "I'm worthless," "I'm helpless," "I'm not wanted," or "I'm not good enough." Validation is your chance to say that what your mate is feeling is important to you, whether those feelings make sense to you or not.

Validation is a little easier than empathy. As a matter of fact, a great deal of healthy validation occurs if you just get good at reflecting back what your spouse is saying. Practice statements like, "So what I hear you saying is . . ." This kind of rephrasing communicates that you are verbally *with* your spouse, on the same page and on the same team.

These reflective statements may also help your spouse clarify his or her feelings. Then you can follow the reflective listening with a simple statement like, "What you are saying matters to me" or "Your feelings are really important" or "It makes sense to me that you are feeling that way." All of those are validating statements.

PRACTICAL WAYS TO CARE FOR YOUR SPOUSE'S HEART

Your spouse has an amazing heart that is the essence of who he or she is, the wellspring of life, the place he or she connects with God, and the place that passes God's blessings on to others (and hopefully you).

You are not responsible for your mate's heart. However, you have an unbelievable opportunity to care for your mate's heart. You probably went so far on your wedding day as to say you would care for your spouse in good times and bad, health and sickness, better or worse, joy or pain. By communicating to understand, allowing compassion to flow, and expressing empathy and validation, you are seizing that opportunity and fulfilling that commitment. You are creating an environment where your spouse can live wholeheartedly. And the best news is that you get to receive the benefits of being married to a wholehearted spouse.

There are a few other ways to care for your spouse's valuable, vulnerable heart:

♡ Support your mate's self-care. An empty, exhausted spouse cannot love wholeheartedly. Notice when your spouse is tired and stressed. Encourage him or her to do things to recharge. Make space for your mate to have some alone time (if you're married to an introvert) or some fellowship time (if you're married to an extravert).

♡ Offer comfort. All people like to have a place where they can curl up, a place they call their own . . . a place where they feel comfortable. Ask your spouse where and what makes him or her feel comfortable. Just like prayer time is a chance for you to climb into the lap of your heavenly Father for comfort, establish a conversation time as a couple that feels comfortable.

In a healthy marriage, you are granted access to the "holy of holies" in your spouse. Prepare yourself, get cleaned up, slip your shoes off so you don't track any mud in, and get in there and care for your mate. Show him or her you care through understanding, compassion, empathy, and validation. Be such a good guest in your spouse's heart that he or she chooses to keep it open. From this place of openness and access, you are free to experience the benefits of a wholehearted marriage.

Chapter 7

Speaking to Your Mate's Heart

Do not let any unwholesome talk come out of your mouths, but only what is helpful for building others up according to their needs, that it may benefit those who listen.

—Ephesians 4:29

A word aptly spoken is like apples of gold in settings of silver.

—Proverbs 25:11

ONE NEW Year's Eve a few years back, we (Shawn and Christina) gathered with a group of about twelve friends. We reviewed the past year together and thought about what was ahead. Someone got around to talking about health and fitness, and then things just started getting out of hand. Next thing I knew, most of us had agreed to train for and run a half marathon (13.1 miles) in the spring.

Up to that point in my life I had run on occasion—mostly

when something was chasing me. But now I was inspired, or at least coerced, by peer pressure.

We chose the Country Music ½ Marathon in Nashville. It was close to us and, even more important, the streets were noted to be lined with people cheering you on and bands playing to add energy. And so we began training. Enthusiasm was high, even if talent was lacking.

Unfortunately, with about a month to go before the big event, I was assigned a work project that would take place on the very weekend of the half marathon. Some of the group had already dropped out because of injuries or because they had come to their senses, but I had really hoped to finish what I started. I decided to continue to train, committing to find another half marathon to bless with my ten-minute-mile (read: just faster than a walk) pace.

The time came, and my friends (the handful still chugging it out) successfully completed the half marathon in Tennessee. I continued to train but could not find another organized race. Finally, I realized I did not have the stamina to continue to train without a goal, nor could my knees continue to agree to take a pounding each morning. I decided to run my own half marathon on a course I set up.

With little fanfare, I left one morning on my route. At the seven-mile mark, I was pleased to see my family stationed with water, signs, and vocal cheering. What an inspiration! My seven-year-old son decided to join me on his bike. Just having him alongside was helpful. I was no longer alone. But even his presence wasn't enough when I began to hit a wall at the nine-mile mark with the sun beating down and no finish line in sight.

Sweat burned my eyes, heat burned my scalp, and fatigue climbed all over me. Desperate for some help, I turned to my son and said, "Cade, I really need some encouragement." For about sixty seconds I continued to pound the pavement, and all I heard was the turning of Cade's peddles. Had he heard me? Surely. He must really be thinking of something profound. When you wait one minute in silence for a reply, your expectations get pretty high.

Then finally, after all the contemplation, came these golden words of inspiration: "Dad, I got nothing."

My internal laughter got me past the wall, and I was able to finish my run. The first, last, and only for me at that distance.

What my friends received with thousands of people cheering them on, and what I did not exactly get when Cade drew a blank, was encouragement.

THE POWER OF ENCOURAGEMENT

Earlier we talked about the role lies and harmful messages play in wounding the heart, eventually leading to shutdown and disconnected marriages. Many of these wounds originate with words spoken from the mouths of people who are significant in our lives. We must recognize our ability to speak to the hearts of those around us—ever conscious that our words can elevate or devastate, help or harm, build up or tear down. For the tongue has the power of life and death (see Proverbs 18:21).

In the last chapter we learned about the value of listening to and caring for the heart of your spouse. But listening is only one part of communication. Speaking is the second part. Your spouse needs not only to be heard but also to be spoken to. The best reflective listener in the world will just seem like a bump on a log if he doesn't ever verbalize an appropriate heart-level response.

What we need are words of encouragement.

To encourage means to infuse with life and energy and courage. The word *encourage* is synonymous with words like buoy, cheer, comfort, and embolden.[1] Does your heart sometimes need to be buoyed, cheered, comforted, and emboldened? Of course it does. And so does your spouse's heart. You have the ability, opportunity, and privilege to speak encouragement into your spouse's heart.

Encouragement could be considered an action (something you do), a talent (something you are gifted with), or a habit (something you develop).

It is true that exhortation is a spiritual gift. Perhaps you have this extraordinary ability from the Lord to encourage others. You are a natural cheerleader. If you are not one, I bet you can think of someone you know who has this gift. Those of us who are not supernaturally gifted to encourage may have to work harder, but we are still capable. Anyone can learn to be encouraging (even my son, Cade).

We challenged one guy I used to work with on his inability to exhort those on his staff. Within a year, he had made a tremendous turn—he wrote emails of praise, verbally affirmed his team, and crafted cards of encouragement at random times for people. The results were a noted improvement in team morale and an increased trust in him as a leader.

Do people really need encouragement? Shouldn't it be enough to just rely on the Lord and believe in ourselves? Yes, you should rely on the Lord. Yes, you should believe in yourself. But no, that is not enough.

Truett Cathy, founder of Chick-fil-A, often asks audiences the following question: "How can you tell if a person needs encouragement?" Cathy pauses, then answers for them: "If they are breathing." We all need encouragement. We all desire to have life spoken into us.

God even took the time to speak encouragement into His

Son. At the start of what most think of as His official ministry, Jesus was baptized by John the Baptist in the Jordan River. As He was coming out of the water, Jesus heard His Father say, "You are my Son, whom I love, with you I am well pleased" (Mark 1:11).

Wouldn't it be nice to start a new job with that kind of affirmation from your heavenly Father? But God did not end His encouragement there. Somewhere in the middle of Jesus' ministry, God took the time to affirm Him in front of His friends. "This is my Son, whom I love. Listen to him!" (Mark 9:7). Sometimes I wish God would affirm me this way in front of my coworkers or family . . . I might get a little more respect.

The point is that if God's Son needed encouragement, your children need encouragement. And your spouse needs encouragement.

Your spouse has a valuable, vulnerable heart. You have the chance to speak to that precious place. We speak to someone's heart through encouragement. Paul wrote, "Do not let any unwholesome talk come out of your mouths, but only what is helpful for building others up according to their needs, that it may benefit those who listen" (Ephesians 4:29).

By encouraging the essence of who your spouse is, you can honor, motivate, and call out the gifting in your mate.

VALUING

Speaking to someone's heart shows value. Kind, encouraging words are a blessing to those who receive them because they build up.

Just the act of heaven being torn open and the voice of the Lord echoing forth was a huge value to Jesus at His baptism. Then add to that God's affirmation that He was well pleased with

Jesus. Remember, this happened before Jesus had really done anything in the way of miracles or recorded ministry. God was valuing who Jesus was, not what He did. God was speaking to Jesus' character, His heart, not His actions or behavior.

We all desire to feel valuable and important. A word aptly spoken to the heart communicates honor and importance. It matters when a boss values you by valuing your work. It matters when a parent values you by affirming you. It matters when a friend values you by praising you. And it matters when your spouse values you through encouragement.

When I (Shawn) was young, I had a coach who valued me with words of praise at a sports banquet. I can still remember how valued I felt the first time I heard my dad say he was proud of me. I can still remember the time a boss valued me by acknowledging my hard work. And I can vividly recall many of the times when my wife has valued me by encouraging and affirming me as a husband.

Face it: you live with your spouse (hopefully). He or she sees all of you: the good, the bad, and the ugly. You want to grant your mate access to your heart. When your spouse is in there, you want him or her to treat it with respect, care, and value.

Think of it this way: Have you ever moved into a new home you were really proud of? If so, did you invite your friends and family over? Remember what you wanted to hear from them? You wanted them to like your place and see the neat things that you liked about it.

Our hearts are similar. We want the people to whom we grant access to look around and like what they see. We want to hear them make nice comments about their experience there.

You want your spouse to say nice things about you—valuable things. Your spouse wants the same thing from you. It's a great feeling to walk up when your spouse is in conversation with someone else and catch him or her praising you. It feels wonderful to hear your spouse look you in the eye and affirm you. It is awesome to be in a marriage where there is no "unwholesome talk" but only words that edify and encourage.

MOTIVATING

Speaking to someone's heart is motivating. A timely word can fuel the confidence someone needs to succeed. Most success stories have a common element: just when the main character needed it most, someone came along with a word of inspiration.

The movie *Rudy* is a classic illustration of our ability to motivate and our ability to destroy with the words we choose. Based on a true story, Rudy is an undersized kid with an oversized dream—to play football at the University of Notre Dame. His father and coaches discourage him by telling him he is too small and too slow. Just when he is prepared to quit and give up on his life aspiration, his mentor and friend inspire him to continue by citing his hard work and determination. Motivated by their words, he gets back on the team. The movie ends with a crowd of people chanting his name and celebrating his accomplishments on the football field.

I recently took eleven-year-old Taylor and eight-year-old Cade canyoneering and rappelling in Arizona. We hiked down into this amazing canyon, squeezing between boulders and climbing over logs. There was a series of about four rock formations that were twenty to thirty feet high. The only way down was to harness in and rappel down the face with a rope to control your pace and stabilize you.

We were having a lot of fun—until we got to the last drop. We looked over the edge and peered out over the canyon floor two hundred feet below. There was no way up or over. The only way out of the canyon was down.

If you could pray your way to having angel wings, Cade would have done it in that moment. He was really scared, and I had only one option: I had to talk him into going over the edge.

"You can do this," I said. "You are so brave. Most eight-year-olds would have quit way back there."

"Right, Dad," he said. "They would be the smart ones."

"Come on, son, courage is not the absence of fear but acting even when you are scared. Besides, if you do this, girls will think you are cool."

It took twenty minutes and a few tears (from both of us), but he was finally willing to step over the edge. We continued a dialogue, and I kept telling him to keep his eyes on me and not look down. He never stopped being scared, but he did get down.

Your words have life-giving power to those around you. Kind, caring, supportive words can inspire a person.

You have a spouse with an amazing heart. The Enemy and the world are trying desperately to make him or her lose heart and give up. At the end of a day your mate's heart may be bloodied and battered. You have the opportunity to come along with words of affirmation and encouragement that breathe life back into him or her. Coming in from a long, tough day at the office, your spouse may need to hear you say, "That company does not know how fortunate they are to have you." Or after a stressful day with small children, you might do well to say, "You are an amazing mom."

One of the goals of a wholehearted marriage is a deep intimate connection with your spouse. Maybe he or she has been closed down for a long time. Maybe you see only glimpses of an opening and only on rare occasions. Encouraging words have a lot of power in situations like this.

When you see a small crack in the wall of your mate's heart, don't just rush in and scare it back closed. Take a moment to affirm the fact that he or she is opening up. If you hear your spouse verbalize a feeling or speak from the heart, let him or her know that you see it and appreciate the effort. Your desire is to get your mate to repeat the behavior, so take a moment to encourage the effort. These little words of affirmation may be the inspiration he or she needs to continue opening.

CALLING OUT GIFTING

Speaking to people's hearts allows you to call out what you see in them. Many people have gifts and talents that they know nothing about. These hidden abilities need to be exposed.

God built gifts into the heart of your spouse that were designed to change the world. You have the unique opportunity to call out that amazing gifting. Like a baseball scout watching a high school game, looking for future talent, you can see things in your spouse that others (and even your spouse) cannot.

The 2008 Summer Olympics focused attention on a swimmer named Michael Phelps. As a gangly, big-eared kid with ADHD, Phelps got very little positive attention growing up. But at age eleven his swim coach saw something special in him. The coach told Phelps's mom that he had the makings of one of the greatest swimmers in history. He saw something in Michael that no one else had seen, and he got to see it come to fruition as Phelps became the only person in history to win eight gold medals in one Olympic Games.

In the book of Judges (chapters 6–7) we learn of a young Jewish man named Gideon. Gideon (not that same guy who puts Bibles in hotel rooms) lived in a time in Israel's history when God was particularly upset with His people. The Jews had turned their backs on God to worship idols, so God decided to give the Promised Land to their enemies (the Midianites). Gideon's people were pushed into the mountains and forced to grow their crops up there. God was so frustrated with His people that He even let the Midianites come and steal the crops and food from the Jews.

As we enter the story, Gideon is in the process of hiding a little bit of wheat that he has just harvested. Out of nowhere, Gideon hears a voice say, "Mighty Warrior." Not knowing who the voice is talking to, Gideon keeps on working. The voice repeats, "Mighty Warrior." Gideon is getting a little frustrated at this point, so he approaches the figure doing the name calling and asks him to hold it down since there are no mighty warriors around. He's trying to hide the wheat without drawing attention.

The figure, who turns out to be an angel of the Lord, says, "I am talking to you, Mighty Warrior." Gideon feels compelled to tell the angel that he has the wrong guy. After all, Gideon is just hiding some food, he is in the weakest family in the tribe, and he is the weakest in his family. Translation: his sister beat him at arm wrestling earlier and that is why he and not she is out here hiding the wheat.

The angel is sure that Gideon is the right guy. Gideon wants proof, so he tests the angel. First, Gideon gets the angel to bring forth fire from a rock for the offering he has brought. Then Gideon puts out a fleece and asks the angel to make the wool wet but the ground around it dry by the next morning. Finally, Gideon wants the angel to make the fleece dry but the ground around it wet by the following morning. Each time, the angel gives Gideon the sign he is looking for.

Gideon begins to trust the angel. So he assembles an army and prepares to take back the Promised Land for his people. Gideon leads the Israelite army to a stunning victory over the enemy. At the end of the day, it was clear: Gideon *was* a mighty warrior.

The temptation is to read the story and say that the angel knew what would happen in the future, so when he called Gideon a mighty warrior, he was simply telling Gideon who he would become. We don't believe that's true. Gideon would not *become* a mighty warrior, he already was one.

When God knit Gideon together in his mother's womb, He made him to be a mighty warrior. Unfortunately, no one had told Gideon. He was going though life with the belief that he was weaker than others. The angel saw the gifting in Gideon's heart and called it out. Gideon then acted in accordance with how he had been designed.

Your spouse was knit together with some amazing gifts, talents, and abilities. Most of the time, however, he or she may not be living and using all of this neat stuff God put inside there. The Enemy has worked to squelch those gifts, rob him or her of those abilities, and convince him or her that those talents are really not that special.

You have an incredible opportunity. You can see into your spouse's heart. You can recognize his or her special talents and abilities. Like the angel of the Lord did with Gideon, you can actually call out that gifting of your spouse. Is your spouse a gifted leader? Tell him. Does your spouse show amazing compassion? Tell her. Is your spouse extraordinary in his or her faith, giving, exhorting, discerning, or wisdom? Why not say so?

Christina loves having parties for people. Early in our marriage, she would often agree to host bridal showers and baby showers. The house would be decorated, food would be prepared, and women would flock into our home. I did my best to vacate the premises.

I was always a little grouchy after these events because I felt like Christina was spending too much money just to throw a party. Could the two hours of playing silly games (like finding out who could make the best wedding dress out of toilet paper) and socializing really be worth the money we were spending? I complained so much that Christina finally stopped hosting these events at our home.

Years later, I learned about the different spiritual gifts. About the same time, I began praying about what it was that made Christina so special to God. It turns out that God had knit Christina together with a special gift of hospitality. My lack of understanding had caused her to stop using her gift, and I felt horrible about it.

We sat down for a heart to heart that was mostly filled with my apologizing and asking forgiveness. I was able to tell Christina that I now recognized the gift of hospitality in her heart and that I wanted to support her in using it however she felt led. She was cautious at first but gradually got back into the swing of hosting parties. Today, Christina is known in our area for making people feel special, warm, welcome, and celebrated. She has opened our home and used her gifting to bless dozens of people.

Because of my access to her heart, I had inadvertently blocked her gifting. And because I finally took the time to look deeper into her heart, I had the opportunity to call out that gifting again.

God freely gives spiritual gifts to His people so that we can serve Him and bless others. Look at the following list of spiritual gifts. Which ones does your spouse have? Don't limit your answers to which ones you see your mate using; also look deeper. Which ones do you think your spouse has that just don't get much outlet?

1. Administration—to govern, pilot, direct, or steer; a
   strategic thinker; manages people and projects well

2. Discernment—a logical ability to think through issues and make good judgments about right and wrong, truth and fiction

3. Encouragement—to comfort, motivate, and give reason for hope; to exhort

4. Faith—an assurance and belief; supernatural trust

5. Giving—to impart, share, deliver, or grant; giving of self with the gift

6. Healing—to effect a cure through God's supernatural power

7. Helping—involvement and interchange where one brings relief and assistance

8. Teaching—excitement around making difficult truths understandable to others

9. Leadership—to rule or preside over by giving vision, direction, and oversight

10. Knowledge—having specific knowledge or insight pertaining to the situation at hand

11. Mercy—compassionate in attitude, word, and action; love in action

12. Miracles—deep sensitivity for God's will and a belief that God can make it happen

13. Prophecy—keen awareness of cultural events and the ability to speak inspirationally about God's place in our culture

14. Service—to aid, relieve, help, or attend to people particularly through the menial duties

15. Wisdom—ability to take truth and apply it intelligently in life situations

In addition to spiritual gifts, God gives us talents and abilities. You can call out these in your spouse too.

A recent branch of psychology has focused its efforts on identifying people's strengths and helping them find appropriate outlets for them. Marcus Buckingham worked for the Gallop Organization, doing extensive survey research. Buckingham found that great managers have the ability to discern the strengths and talents of employees.[2] He even compiled a test to identify people's strengths.[3]

You don't need fancy research measures to tell you what your spouse is good at. Just look into his or her heart. What do you see? What brings your mate alive? What talents does he or she use that really make a difference in your family or the lives of others around you? What do you hear other people affirm about your spouse? Take some time to ponder these questions. Then get busy encouraging your spouse by calling out the gifts, talents, and abilities that are etched in his or her heart.

SPEAKING YOUR SPOUSE'S HEART LANGUAGE

Okay, so you are starting to believe that there is some value in encouraging your spouse. You recognize that your mate has a valuable, vulnerable heart that you get a chance to care for. Now you want to say something meaningful.

Imagine getting a chance to meet the ruler of a foreign land. If you are at all conscientious, you would want to know a little about this people's customs and how they greet each other in their culture. You would want to show honor by acting appropriately in their presence. You would want to communicate something recognizable and valuable.

The same is true of speaking to your spouse's heart. You want to say something that is honoring and meaningful. So do the same kind of respectful research. Find out what your spouse needs to hear and say it. Study your mate to determine what the heart-level needs are and speak to those. Ephesians 4:29 tells us to "Build others up *according to their needs.*" This requires you to first know what your spouse's heart-level needs are, then build them up accordingly.

How do you determine heart-level needs? Glad you asked. Here are some suggestions.

First, think back to the discussion of fears, lies, and messages. Can you think of any of the wounds your spouse has experienced? What fears or messages were received? As we discussed in chapter 3, a person's deepest desires and wants are usually the exact opposite of his or her deepest fears. That is the way the Enemy works: if you have a desire, he is going to line up a fear right next to it. Therefore if you know your spouse's fears you can also take a pretty good guess about his or her deepest desires. Look at the list below and the corresponding heart desires.

The list below shows how fears are really the opposite of our desires, and vice versa.

Fear of Being	Corresponding Desire for Being
Rejected	Accepted
Abandoned	Committed
Disconnected	Connected
Failed	Successful
Helpless	In control
Powerless	Powerful
Inadequate	Adequate

Fear of Being	Corresponding Desire for Being
Inferior	Self-confident
Invalidated	Validated
Unloved	Loved
Undesirable	Desirable
Not good enough	Good enough
Worthless	Worthy
Devalued	Valued
Unaccepted	Approved of
Judged	In grace
Ignored	Regarded
Unimportant	Important, worthy
Intimate	Safe
Misunderstood	Understood
Wrongly portrayed	Truthfully portrayed
Disrespected	Respected
Unwanted	Wanted
Defective	Accepted

You know your fears. What would it feel like to hear your spouse speak the corresponding desire into your heart?

I (Shawn) have a fear of rejection, which means I also have a deep desire for acceptance. A few years back, my dad was in the audience for the first time to hear me speak on marriage. I talked about the heart and feelings—and the entire time I was wondering what the old cowboy was thinking. After I finished, Dad took me out to dinner. Sitting across the table, he intentionally caught my eye and said, "Son, I am so proud of you." Wow, I felt his acceptance of me and my profession and my performance. I felt his love.

We all long for this type of affirmation. You do, and so does your spouse. Your words have healing power when you speak directly to your mate's heart desires.

Our second suggestion to help you discover your spouse's heart-level needs is to ask your mate.

David Ferguson, founder of Intimate Life Ministries, uses the term *intimacy* to refer to heart-level connection. In *Intimate Encounters*[4] Ferguson lists what he considers to be our top-ten intimacy needs:

1. Acceptance: receiving another person willingly and unconditionally when the other's behavior has been imperfect. Being willing to continue loving another in spite of offenses (Romans 15:7).

2. Affection: expressing care and closeness through physical touch; saying "I love you" (Romans 16:16; Mark 10:16).

3. Appreciation: expressing thanks, praise, or commendation. Recognizing accomplishment or effort (Colossians 3:15; 1 Corinthians 11:2).

4. Approval (blessing): building up or affirming another; affirming both the fact of and the importance of a relationship (Ephesians 4:29; Mark 1:11).

5. Attention: conveying appropriate interest, concern, and care; taking thought of another; entering another's "world" (1 Corinthians 12:25).

6. Comfort: responding to a hurting person with words, feelings, and touch; to hurt with and for another's grief or pain (Romans 12:15); Matthew 5:4; 2 Corinthians 1:3–4; John 11:35).

7. Encouragement: urging another to persist and persevere toward a goal; stimulating toward love and good deeds (1 Thessalonians 5:11; Hebrews 10:24).

8. Respect: valuing and regarding another highly; treating another as important; honoring another (Romans 12:10).

9. Security (peace): harmony in relationships; freedom from fear or threat of harm (Romans 12:16, 18).

10. Support: coming alongside and gently helping with a problem or struggle, providing appropriate assistance (Galatians 6:2).

First, how well did your mom do at giving you these things when you were growing up? Did she manage to communicate high levels of acceptance, affection, appreciation, etc? Second, how well did your dad do at communicating and meeting each need when you were growing up?

It would be fairly common for you to review the list and realize that your parents were good at addressing some of these intimacy needs for you and not so good at others. Maybe you grew up in a home where one of your parents was absent physically or where he or she was present but not emotionally skilled to speak into any of these needs.

Perhaps you're jumping ahead and thinking about how *your* kids would say you are doing. Don't go there yet. You want to be a good parent, but stay focused on yourself for a moment.

At your current age and place in life, which of the intimacy needs on the list are most important to you? If you had to narrow it to just two, which two would you want to tell your spouse you need the most?

Have your spouse look at the same list. Ask about how well these needs were met for him or her growing up. Ask what his or her top two would be right now. Get really practical with each other. If he or she says, "Respect and attention are the two needs I want most from you," then ask for some practical ways you could communicate that respect and some practical ways that would make him or her feel like you are showing attention. Share your top two with your mate and give practical suggestions on how to communicate those to you.

Talking about our intimacy needs is a great avenue into someone's heart. These are heart-level needs. Food and shelter are examples of physical needs. Time with God and fellowship with other believers are spiritual needs. Acceptance, affection, appreciation, and the others on the list are heart-level emotional needs.

Couples who understand these needs and know how to speak to each other on this level have wholehearted marriages. Not knowing these needs or ignoring them leads to feelings of neglect.

In the worst cases, people go to people outside of the marriage to get these needs met. This can potentially spiral forward into an emotional affair and eventually something physical. Don't let that be the story of your marriage. Seek to understand the intimacy needs of your spouse and make intentional efforts to speak to this important place in his or her heart.

A third way to speak directly to your spouse's heart is to know and communicate through his or her love language. Gary Chapman did us all a service when he identified and wrote about the different ways we can communicate love to each other. In his book *The Five Love Languages*[5] Chapman explains five different channels we can use to get love from one heart to another. As you read the following, think about which of the five you would most like to receive from your spouse:

- ♡ Words of Affirmation—Verbal compliments and encouraging words like we have been describing. For example, Jesus was affirmed by a voice from heaven.

- ♡ Quality Time—Undivided attention, togetherness, quality conversation focused on listening, and quality activities. For example, Jesus often spent time alone with the disciples for instruction and fellowship.

- ♡ Gifts—Visual symbols of love. For example, Jesus accepted the gift of the woman's perfume and washing of His feet.

- ♡ Acts of Service—Doing things or performing duties you know your spouse would like you to do. For example, Jesus washed the disciples' feet.

- ♡ Physical Touch—Hugging, holding hands, kissing, walking arm in arm. For example, Jesus was willing to touch the lepers and hold the little children.

A simple key to understanding love languages is to imagine you have a love tank (like a gas tank in your car). If you are like most, one or two of the love languages will speak directly to you and fill your tank. The other three or four areas are likely to do very little in terms of making you feel loved. By identifying your love language and communicating it to your spouse, you give your mate an opportunity to express love in a way that will consistently hit the mark. You will feel loved and your spouse will feel successful.

In the same way, you have the opportunity to identify your spouse's love languages and work to fill his or her love tank.

As a warning, know that very few spouses have the same love language. I found this out the hard way in the early going with my wife. She had school until late at night, so I would spend that time washing clothes, cooking dinner, and cleaning our home for her. She would come in and hardly even notice. My feelings were hurt. It took me a long time to realize that while I felt loved when someone performed acts of service (and therefore was expressing love to her by doing acts of service for her), this language did very little for her.

In much the same way, I would go on trips occasionally and find cards from my wife stuck in my suitcase. While those cards did little for me personally, they did teach me that my wife spoke the language of words of affirmation. I am now more conscious of affirming her, and she is better at doing things for me. In this way, we get the love in our hearts over to each other.

If you are connected to God, you can rest assured that you have plenty of love in your heart. Your job is to give that love away to your spouse. The more you understand about your mate's heart, the better you are going to be at getting love over to him or her. Knowing your spouse's heart desires, heart needs, and love language is an amazing start.

When I was younger, I collected baseball cards. Each card had a picture on the front and a lot of statistics about the player on the back. I have since outgrown the baseball cards, but I still carry one significant picture in my wallet. In a sense, it is my wife's baseball card. It has her picture on the front and her stats on the back. Not her height and weight (never write that down where someone else can see it), but her heart statistics. I have her heart desires, heart needs, and love language right on the back as a reminder to me. (I also have the phone number of the florist for the times I have neglected the other three categories.)

A wholehearted marriage is characterized by communication that is meant for building up each other and targeted to speak a language that will be received by your spouse.

CAN YOU HEAR ME?

One final point about heart-level communication. In any good communication, two things are needed: talking and listening; sending and receiving. Knowing each other's hearts will certainly help you be more successful in sending communication that is meaningful and hearable. However, speaking to each other's hearts is only fully effective when the receiving is as good as the sending. Many of us fall short when it comes to receiving heart-level communication, affirmation, and encouragement from others.

The first problem occurs when you are speaking to a person's heart that is closed. No matter how well chosen your words and delivery system, you cannot force someone to open. But don't give up. Life-giving, positive, affirming, desire-meeting communication will make a person feel safer and does have the power to open an otherwise closed heart. As Proverbs 12:25 tells us, an anxious (fearful) heart weighs a man down, but a kind word cheers him up. Your kind affirming words will create a safe environment that will allow your spouse's heart to open.

A second reception problem occurs when the receiver has an open heart but does not know how to respond to encouragement.

Many people are prone to demonstrate a form of false humility in which they intentionally deflect compliments and praise. Have you ever complimented people only to hear them respond,

"Well, God gets all the credit for that" or "That's just what my mother taught me to do" or "I just got lucky"?

We have any number of ways to deflect praise. That "giving God all the credit" one really makes us sound holy and spiritual. But you don't have to do that. God knows His contribution; He doesn't need your affirmation or credit. He actually delights in seeing His children use their gifting and get praised for displaying their talents.

Try this exercise our friends Nathan and Jane taught us. The next time someone affirms you, say, "I receive that." Don't deflect the credit, minimize the accomplishment, or otherwise avoid receiving the blessing the person is trying to give you. Just receive it. With an open heart, let your spouse speak life into you. Ask him or her to offer you the same opportunity.

Well-sent and well-received words can transform a marriage from halfhearted to wholehearted. You have the ability to speak life into your spouse's heart—honoring, motivating, and inspiring your mate.

Imagine what it must have felt like for Peter to hear Jesus refer to him as a rock on which He would build His church (see Matthew 16:18). Calling out Peter's gifting that way must have reverberated in Peter's heart later as he did indeed found the early church, enjoying exciting success and facing painful persecution.

What an awesome power and privilege we have to speak to the hearts of those around us. You communicate love by speaking to your spouse's heart. Taking the time to understand your mate's heart desires, needs, and language shows you care. Using these avenues to communicate says "I love you" at the deepest level. You have a chance to be your spouse's most fierce ally, steadfast friend, and faithful companion. Don't shirk your duty. Have a wholehearted marriage by boldly speaking life and truth into each other.

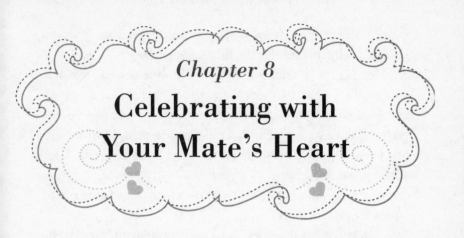

Chapter 8
Celebrating with Your Mate's Heart

A cheerful heart is good medicine, but a crushed spirit dries up the bones.

—Proverbs 17:22

Laughter is the shortest distance between two people.

—Victor Borge

ENJOY LIFE with the woman whom you love all the days of your fleeting life which He has given to you under the sun; for this is your reward in life" (Ecclesiastes 9:9 NASB). This great advice was written by King Solomon around the year 935 B.C. Even thousands of years ago, people were able to realize the importance of spending time enjoying their spouses.

Over the years I (Greg) have done my best to follow Solomon's wise counsel as closely as possible. And, unfortunately for Erin, she is often the target of my attempts at fun and enjoyment. I think it's safe to say that Erin is married to a joker. I can see the funny side of almost anything, even in the dead of night or when disaster strikes. I'm always playing practical jokes on Erin. So Erin was delighted the day she finally got payback.

Her plan was simple yet extremely mischievous. She was going to hide in a dark corner of our back entryway and ambush me as I walked in the house from the garage. I must admit it was perfect. While some people don't like to be scared, I thrive on it. She knew I'd find her stunt hilarious—and she'd get me back for all my practical jokes.

The garage door lifted slowly as my Honda Civic approached after a long day at work.

Erin giggled as she hid in the corner, awaiting my arrival. She remained perfectly still as the door opened.

I took two steps in and then noticed a dark, sinister figure standing near my left shoulder. At that moment Erin grabbed my arm and screamed. Startled, I let out a shrieking yelp and flew back into the door.

"Revenge is so sweet!" Erin yelled as I massaged my pounding heart. We exchanged high-fives and embraced. "Welcome home!" Erin said, as we both laughed.

You have to respect (and fear) a woman who planned so meticulously to scare her husband. I have to keep reminding her that I'm getting old and my heart isn't as strong as it once was.

After Erin and I settled into a quiet evening, I began to reflect on the fact that one of my favorite things about our marriage is the fun we have together. I smiled as I thought about Erin's vicious and unprovoked prank and the joy it gave her to scare me. The best part was realizing how Erin's little practical joke actually helped me feel connected to her. Who knew that being scared half to death could turn into emotional intimacy?

During our seventeen years of marriage Erin and I have discovered that having fun together is one of the keys to a great marriage. One of the things that first attracted me to Erin was her ability to make me laugh. Our laughter brought me joy during our courtship, and it continues to bring me happiness all these years later.

STRENGTHENING YOUR MARRIAGE BY HAVING *FUN*

Humor in marriage has always fascinated me. As I researched what the experts had to say about fun and laughter in marriage, I was overwhelmed by its importance.

For example, marital-research experts Dr. Scott Stanley, Dr. Howard Markman, and Dr. Susan Blumberg conducted a survey to discover what creates a strong relationship. To their surprise, the amount of fun couples had together emerged as the strongest factor in understanding overall marital happiness. Other positives were occurring in these relationships—but good relationships became great when they were preserving both the quantity and quality of fun times together.[1]

In her excellent book *Traits of a Healthy Family*, Dolores Curran makes this observation about healthy families:

The primary hallmark of a strong family seems to be its absence of guilt at times of play. Individuals and the family collectively give themselves permission to sit back, relax, dream, and enjoy. Further, they schedule play times onto the calendar; they don't wait for free time.[2]

If laughter is the best medicine, most of us haven't gotten the prescription filled. Adults laugh only about seventeen times a day, compared to preschool-age children, who laugh about three hundred times a day.[3] The sad truth is that many couples no longer share the type of fun they had when they were dating or newly married. It's almost as though the daily grind of life has zapped their ability and/or desire to have fun together.

It certainly makes sense. Keeping up with jobs, kids, church, and friends makes it increasingly difficult to find time together. Throw conflict into the pot, and you have the perfect environment for removing the fun from life.

This is so unfortunate, because God created the gift of fun and laughter to be used in our relationships. It was all His idea. There are plenty of verses in the Bible that show God's sense of humor and the power of laughter:

- ♡ He will yet fill your mouth with laughter and your lips with shouts of joy. (Job 8:21)
- ♡ A time to weep and a time to laugh, a time to mourn and a time to dance. (Ecclesiastes 3:4)
- ♡ A cheerful heart is good medicine, but a crushed spirit dries up the bones. (Proverbs 17:22)
- ♡ A cheerful look brings joy to the heart, and good news gives health to the bones. (Proverbs 15:30)

What God has clearly ordained and what our grandparents intuitively understood—that laughter is good medicine—researchers have only recently begun to study.

LAUGHTER IS THE BEST MEDICINE

Most couples understand the value of a good relationship. Advice on how to make a marriage work fills bookstore shelves and plays incessantly on radio and TV talk shows. But of all the factors that contribute to a good relationship, there is one that seldom gets translated into advice or even therapy: *laughter*.

Fun and laughter may be exactly what our marriages need most. For hundreds of years, people have claimed that laughter is the best medicine. New scientific research is helping us understand the benefits of humor on our health and well-being. Laughter has a powerful effect. Whether it's for dealing with the pressures of daily life, stress, or even an illness, laughter can dramatically change the quality and outlook of our lives. And laughing makes us feel good for a reason.

Joe and his wife are out in the woods hunting when Joe keels over. Frantic, Joe's wife dials 911 and blurts, "My husband just dropped dead! What should I do?"

A soothing voice at the other end says, "Don't worry, I can help. First, let's make sure he's really dead."

After a brief silence, the operator hears a shot. Then Joe's wife comes back to the phone. "Okay," she says nervously to the operator, "what do I do next?"

Didn't it feel good to laugh? Whether or not you thought that was funny, the physiological effects of laughter are pretty amazing. Here are some examples of the impact of laughter on the body. Laughter:

- ♡ lowers your blood pressure and decreases heart strain by increasing dopamine levels;
- ♡ reduces stress hormones that constrict blood vessels and suppress immune activity;
- ♡ boosts your immune system and helps combat upper respiratory infections;
- ♡ helps tone facial muscles and nourishes the skin;
- ♡ triggers the release of endorphins—the body's natural painkillers;

♡ protects the stomach from forming ulcers;

♡ improves your body's ability to use oxygen by empting your lungs of more air than it takes in. This results in a cleansing effect similar to deep breathing;

♡ promotes healing; even in the most difficult of times a laugh, or even simply a smile, can go a long way in helping us feel better;

♡ produces a general sense of well-being.[4]

All this means a stronger immune system as well as fewer physical effects of stress. Laughter even exercises the diaphragm, by contracting the abs, and works out the shoulders, leaving muscles more relaxed afterward. Researchers say laughter speeds up the heart rate so it provides a good aerobic workout for the heart. As a matter of fact, laughing a hundred times is the equivalent to ten minutes on the rowing machine or fifteen minutes on an exercise bike.

And if the aerobic benefits aren't enticing enough, according to the British Dental Health Foundation, a smile gives the same level of stimulation as eating two thousand chocolate bars. I wonder how many Starbucks lattes that would equal?

The best news of all is that laughing for fifteen seconds a day adds two days to a person's overall lifespan.[5] With as much as I laugh, I should live until I'm 138 years old!

Laughter is free and has no known negative side effects. Laughter has an amazing impact on our physical health and well-being, but the true benefit is what humor does to your marriage.

THE IMPACT OF FUN AND LAUGHTER ON YOUR MARRIAGE

What is it about laughing with your spouse that feels so good? Is it the telling of a joke or funny story that's so rewarding? Or is it the fact that someone actually finds you funny? Does it have something to do with the punch line or your clever wit? None of those truly matters. The real relational benefit of humor is how *safe* it feels to be in the presence of someone who is laughing.

Now, I'm not talking about when someone laughs "at" you or uses you as the punch line of a joke. These things are dishonoring and lead to your feeling unsafe. Instead, I'm talking about laughing "with" your spouse.

Laughter feels safe because it opens your heart. It's impossible to have a closed heart and laugh at the same time. This is why when our children are in a bad mood, nothing works better than a quick tickle or funny joke to get them laughing and in a better place emotionally. A monk named Yogi Raman said it best: "Laughter opens your heart and soothes your soul." And then there's Victor Borge's great quote: "Laughter is the shortest distance between two people."

But why is this true? The answer is pretty amazing. Since humor helps to make a person feel emotionally safe and keeps the heart open, laughter actually enhances people's ability to connect with others. When people laugh together, it unites and binds them closer together.

At a conference I attended recently I was with a large group listening to the plenary speaker, when I noticed the most interesting behavior. The scene was a few hundred strangers crammed together around a bunch of small tables. No one was really interacting, and the mood felt awkward. That is, until the speaker

239

shared a joke. As laughter spread out across the room, people instantly looked at one another and nodded approvingly.

I had been in large groups many times before, but I had never paid attention to how people interact around humor. Here you had a group of awkward strangers who, seconds before, had been hardly interacting. And then the moment the speaker shared something funny, the entire room united. You could literally feel the uneasiness melt away. It was amazing.

Humor has this effect on people. When two people hear something funny, they seek out the gaze of another person. Why? It's quite simple really: they want connection with others. Laughter can establish—or restore—a positive emotional climate and a sense of connection between two people. We take pleasure in the company of another person when exposed to humor. In fact, the health benefits of laughter may result from the social support it stimulates. Thus, laughter may not be primarily about humor; instead, it may be about relationships.[6]

There are actually a whole host of ways that fun and laughter bring a married couple together and promote intimacy and connection. Consider these:

- ♡ Laughter is contagious and helps generate more laughter. Studies show that people laugh far more when they are with other people than when they are alone, and laughter flows most freely when people feel comfortable with one another.
- ♡ The stress in our lives from work, household responsibilities, children, and the demands of society can feel overwhelming at times. After a long day, a home environment filled with laughter eases stress levels significantly. By elevating the mood of your spouse, you can diminish his or her stress levels

and improve the quality of the interaction you experience together, reducing your stress level even more!

♡ A simple smile or a giggle can break the ice when things are tense. Humor lightens our burdens and helps us keep things in perspective. This "halo effect" helps couples remember other happy events more vividly and feel more optimistic and positive toward each other.

♡ Having a sense of humor helps keep your relationship fresh and can ease the mundane times of marriage. This adds life to your marriage and produces a general sense of well-being that lifts your spirits.

♡ People look younger and more approachable when they laugh. This creates a relaxed kind of intimacy. Scientists have found that mutual laughter helps people feel at ease around each other. This sets a peaceful tone in your marriage.

♡ The use of humor can catch your spouse's attention and has the capacity to hold it. Ladies can now have no excuse for saying their husbands never listen to them—they just have to make it funny![7]

All things considered, healthy humor can open hearts and bring a married couple closer. It is playful, increases intimacy, reduces stress, and increases positive emotions. If your relationship could use a little jump start, add in some fun and laughter.

ADDING FUN AND LAUGHTER
TO YOUR MARRIAGE

Life is so stressful. We get caught up in our careers, children, obligations, chauffeuring the kids, sitting in bleachers watching our children play, answering emails, making meetings, handling the finances, and scheduling appointments. By the time evening arrives, both spouses are often exhausted and in need of some alone time.

Obviously this hinders our ability to enjoy each other. We often get so busy doing life that we forget that laughing and having fun together is as important as discussing our frustrations and hurts, paying our bills, and getting the household chores done. In fact, without the ability to have fun, our time together becomes synonymous with strenuous labor.

Introducing a little lightheartedness into your relationship may be just the thing you need to rejuvenate your marriage. Here are four quick tips to bring some fun and laughter into your relationships.

Fun Tip #1: Turn Toward Your Spouse

As a certain young boy opened up a Christmas present, he found a note from his father inside the small box. "Son, this year I will give you 365 hours, an hour every day after dinner." "This simple present became the greatest gift I ever had in my life," explained the boy as an adult. "Because my dad not only kept his promise, but every year he renewed it. I am the result of his time."[8]

If you can devote that kind of time to having fun with your spouse, a wholehearted marriage will be the result. One of the most important aspects of relating in marriage is to "turn toward" each other. When you turn toward your spouse, you express interest, attention, and curiosity. Marriage researcher Dr. John Gottman coined the phrase "turn toward each other" to describe this kind of behavior between couples.[9] When you turn toward each other, you literally shift your focus and fix your eyes on your spouse.

You acknowledge your husband's entrance and ask, "How was your day?" when he walks in the door instead of keeping your eyes glued to whatever you were doing. You engage your wife at the grocery store, "Aren't we almost out of milk?" instead of thinking about the football game. You give your husband a quick kiss on the chin when he peers over your shoulder. You smile and give your wife a quick look to connect in some small way over your morning coffee. Even in brief exchanges like these, husband and wife choose to turn toward each other instead of away.

Why is turning toward each other so vital? Because it helps love mature and prevents conflict from infiltrating the relationship. Gottman has studied hundreds of couples, and he's found that loving, romantic relationships are not maintained through vacation getaways and lavish gifts. Instead, happy couples keep their love alive through small, everyday acts. They talk to each other, laugh together, and pay attention to what the other is doing and saying. In small ways they turn toward each other instead of ignoring or turning away.[10]

I saw the importance of this "turning toward" when my daughter, Taylor, was three and kept making the most unusual request: "Daddy, would you please play like you're a little doggie?"

For several months, these were the words that greeted me as I returned home from work. Instead of wanting me to play with her toys or read a book, Taylor wanted me to get down on all fours and bark like a dog. At first, I thought this request was cute. But as a psychologist, my concern slowly began to surface. Was this canine fixation normal? Should I consult a child therapist—or a veterinarian?

I thought about this for several weeks and even asked other fathers if their children wanted them to be dogs. To my surprise, several dads relayed similar experiences. The situation continued to puzzle me until I picked up Taylor from daycare one day.

Walking into the daycare, I heard several children laughing uncontrollably in the next room. The laughter was intoxicating, and I found myself smiling at the anticipation of learning what was so funny. Entering the playroom, I quickly understood the reason for their laughter. A small puppy was chasing Taylor until she fell to the ground. Once on her back, the puppy began licking her face until it dripped with puppy saliva. (I'm not sure that would have made *me* laugh—gag maybe.)

Tucked in a corner, away from Taylor's view, I stood there watching my daughter have so much fun. Her laughter was contagious, and I found myself smiling. However, I also felt a strange sense of jealousy. Seeing the excitement in her eyes, I began to wonder if I made Taylor that happy when we played together. Suddenly, I found myself watching the puppy. What was that little ball of fur doing that Taylor enjoyed so much?

Like a ton of bricks hitting me on the head, I finally understood. As they played, the puppy was completely focused on my daughter. He wasn't thinking about other dogs, his next meal, finding a shoe to chew on, or attacking the neighbor's cat. The puppy had only one focus: *playing with Taylor.*

No wonder my daughter wished I was a dog. She needed undivided attention from me. Taylor wanted to look into my eyes and find me completely focused on her. Instead of my playing with her during TV commercials or while working or doing household tasks, Taylor wanted to feel like the most important thing at that moment. She wanted me to turn toward her.

In Gottman's experience, "couples who turn toward each other remain emotionally engaged and stay married." He says that "turning toward is the basis of emotional connection, romance, passion, and a good sex life."[11] Who would turn down that list? Simply put, spouses turning toward each other helps love grow and helps prevent drifting apart.

Here are some ideas to help you turn toward your spouse:

♡ Make an effort to do everyday activities *together.* Fold the laundry together, clean the house together, pay bills together, do yard work together, and cook dinner together.

♡ Pray *with* your spouse (mealtimes don't count!).

♡ Go on a fun date.

♡ Dream about your future together.

♡ Find a fun activity you both like, such as bowling, bicycling, hiking, jogging, horseback riding, fishing, camping, canoeing, sailing, water skiing, or swimming.

♡ Regularly share with each other what God is teaching you in your individual spiritual journeys.

♡ Acknowledge each other when your spouse returns home or enters a room.

♡ Reunite at the end of the day and talk about your highs and lows.

♡ Listen to praise and worship music together.

♡ Find time to talk without interruptions so you can truly listen to each other.

♡ Attend a marriage seminar every year.

♡ If you enjoy puzzles, work on one together.

♡ Call each other in the middle of the day just to say "I love you" and "I miss you."

♡ Find a TV show that you both enjoy watching.

♡ Regularly attend church together and share a pen to take notes.

♡ Cuddle up on a cozy couch or on the patio to talk about nonserious matters.

♡ Read a book aloud together.

♡ Show genuine interest while your spouse talks; stay focused on him or her. You can let him or her know you're truly present by nodding, smiling, grimacing, and asking for details.

♡ Cofacilitate a marriage small group or teach a Bible study together.

♡ Express affection. Hold, touch, and embrace your mate. Say "I love you" often.

♡ Make up a grocery list and go shopping together.

♡ Pray *for* your spouse.

♡ Read the morning paper together.

♡ Help each other with self-improvement plans, such as a new class, weight loss, exercise, a new career.

♡ Schedule a regular lunch together during the workweek.

♡ Go on a picnic or road trip to have some "windshield" time.

♡ Shop together for gifts or for the kids' clothing.

♡ Talk or read together by an open fire.

♡ Sit next to each other at your child's sporting events or performances.

♡ Take kids to the doctor, dentist, teacher conferences, lessons, and other mundane appointments together.

♡ Read the Bible or some other type of spiritual book together to strengthen your walk with the Lord.

♡ Drive to or from work together.

♡ Play a board game or a card game.

♡ Volunteer together at a local not-for-profit ministry or organization.

♡ Have a family devotional time.

Another key is to realize that your time together doesn't have to be extensive. Actually, it needs to be only about twenty minutes per day.

Dr. Gottman discovered through his research that the difference between a couple who divorces and one that stays together, but is unhappy, is that the latter spends ten minutes a day of turning toward each other and the former spends less than that. Furthermore, Gottman found that couples who stay together and are *happy* turn toward each other an additional ten minutes each day more than unhappily married couples.

From these discoveries we conclude that a total of twenty minutes a day of turning toward each other in substantial ways can make the difference between divorce and staying together in a happy, satisfying relationship.[12]

Will you invest at least twenty minutes turning toward your spouse every day through positive words or affirmative interactions?

Fun Tip #2: Surprise Your Spouse by Doing Something Unexpected

For weeks a certain married couple had been debating the purchase of a new auto. He wanted a new truck. She wanted a fast little sports car. The more they looked, the more they couldn't seem to agree. He would probably have settled on any beat-up old truck, but everything she seemed to like was way out of their price range.

"Look!" she said, "I want something that goes from zero to two hundred in four seconds or less. And my birthday is coming up. Why don't you surprise me?"

So for her birthday, her husband bought her a brand-new bathroom scale.

Services will be at Downing Funeral Home on Monday. Due to the condition of the body, this will be a closed-casket service. Please send your donations to the Think Before You Buy Stupid Things for Your Wife's Birthday Foundation.

Although we can marvel at this husband's daring, this isn't exactly the type of surprise we're talking about. As the years go by, many couples slip into a rut of predictability. Things that used to excite and thrill don't produce the same reaction they used to. And when a marriage becomes predictable or routine, the passion diminishes. Couples slowly begin to drift apart emotionally.

This dulls the love feeling that you once had. Spouses begin to feel disenchanted and disillusioned in their marriages. They start to think, *This isn't what I thought marriage was going to be like. I didn't sign up for this!* This disappointment often leads to a slow disconnection and creates feelings of isolation and loneliness. And when people feel lonely in their marriages, they usually turn to other people and things (e.g., work, children, friends, hobbies, etc.) to experience connection and excitement.

But your marriage does not have to become predictable or routine. In order to keep the excitement and passion in a marriage, a husband and wife must make time for the unexpected. Anything unexpected that breaks your daily routine is ideal. Why is this so important? Let us tell you about some amazing new research.

Many couples schedule a weekly date night—a regular evening out with friends or alone together at a favorite restaurant to strengthen their marital bond. But brain and behavior research- ers say many couples are going about date night all wrong. Sim- ply spending quality time together is probably not enough to prevent a relationship from getting stale.

Most studies show that the decline of romantic love over time is inevitable in a marriage. The butterflies of early romance quickly flutter away and are replaced by familiar, predictable feel- ings of long-term attachment. But several experiments show that simply doing new things together as a couple may help bring the butterflies back, recreating the chemical surges of early court- ship. Using laboratory studies, real-world experiments, and even brain scan data, scientists can now offer married couples a simple prescription for rekindling the romantic love that brought them together in the first place.

The solution? Reinventing date night.

Rather than visiting the same familiar places and dining with the same old friends, couples need to tailor their date nights around new and different activities that they both enjoy. The goal is to find ways to keep injecting newness and freshness into the marriage. The activity can be as simple as trying a new restaurant or something a little more unusual or thrilling—like taking an art class or going to an amusement park.[13]

Try these ideas to surprise each other and bring some fresh- ness to your marriage:

- ♡ Hide a little note in a lunch or briefcase that says "I love you" or "I'm proud of you."
- ♡ Create private jokes between you and your spouse that only you understand. It's great when you give each other "the look" and smile and acknowledge the secret joke.

♡ Bring home flowers or a box of candy, just like you did when you were dating.

♡ Play practical jokes on each other or (gently) scare your spouse.

♡ Go dancing or attend a concert, nightclub, jazz club, or theater.

♡ Try a scavenger hunt. One husband taped a note for his wife on the door. The note led her to numerous other notes until she discovered her husband in the closet holding a "pot of gold" (her cooking kettle with a gift inside it).

♡ Take a moonlight walk or get up early to exercise together.

♡ Stay overnight at a romantic hideaway.

♡ Hide little cute messages around the house.

One couple did this by writing the word "shmily" in a surprise place for the other to find. They would take turns leaving "shmily" around the house, and as soon as the other discovered it, it was that person's turn to hide it.

They dragged "shmily" with their fingers through the sugar and flour containers to await whoever was preparing the next meal. "Shmily" was written in the steam left on the mirror after a hot shower, where it would reappear bath after bath. At one point, one of them even unrolled and then rerolled an entire roll of toilet paper to leave "shmily" on the very last sheet. There is no end to the creative places "shmily" can pop up! What does "shmily" mean? S-H-M-I-L-Y: See How Much I Love You.

♡ Develop pet names for each other.

♡ Lovingly tease each other. Tell your husband he's looking "mighty hot" in those Levis or mismatched outfit. Whistle at your wife and ask, "Hey, baby, where you been all my life?" However, be careful with your teasing. Erin and I have a rule that you can never joke about something that the other person can't change. Don't say, "It's not the clothes that make you look fat; it's the fat that makes you look fat!" If you're the partner being teased—and if it was done with love—laugh.

♡ Talk in a funny accent or learn to say "I love you" in different languages.

♡ Don't take yourself too seriously. Learn from your mistakes and then move on. Taking yourself less seriously enables you to laugh at your mistakes and learn from them instead of stewing about them and letting them ruin your day.

♡ Play games or cards together like Yahtzee or Dutch Blitz.

♡ Do some playful sparring: a little love tap on the arm, followed by one to the chin, and then start to bob and weave . . . just be playful.

♡ Tell each other jokes or funny stories.

♡ Take turns hiding a little plastic red heart in places where your spouse is sure to find it. Every time you find it, the message is that you are loved. But don't get too good at hiding the heart because it could stay hidden for a long time.

♡ Pull your shorts up to your armpits, make a funny face, and ask for a big hug.

♡ Play video games together. The Nintendo Wii is one of the best marriage investments we've made in a long time. If you have one, then you know what I'm talking about. If you don't, get one.

251

♡ Share funny things that happened throughout the day.

♡ Be playful around mistakes. If your partner is a little short with you, instead of berating him, say in a lighthearted way, "Where's the love, baby? I'm not feelin' the love." Since you'll most likely laugh at your mistakes someday, anyway, why not laugh at them now?

♡ Collect funny cards or cartoons you know your spouse would enjoy.

♡ Surprise your spouse with an unexpected gesture of affection (although I've heard that most women don't consider a slap on the backside a gesture of affection!).

♡ Watch a funny movie or romantic comedy together. *America's Funniest Home Videos* seldom fails to make us laugh. I always feel closer to Erin when we're laughing together.

You don't have to get crazy, make elaborate plans, or spend a lot of money to be spontaneous and do something unexpected. Doing almost anything that is just the two of you—no kids, no telephone, no other commitments or obligations—will go a long way toward reminding you of why you got married in the first place.

Speaking of why you got married, read this next tip.

Fun Tip #3: Reminisce About Memorable Things That Have Happened over the Course of Your Marriage

I was at work when Erin called me, weeping. "Oprah was doing a show on love stories," she said, "and I just watched the most amazing love story I've ever seen. Ever!"

"I thought our story was the best," I joked.

"You've got to come home and watch this story with me," Erin said, begging.

I must admit that I sat on the couch with my wife that night and cried my eyes out. I was blown away by a young Polish man's story of how he fell in love with his wife.

When Herman Rosenblat was twelve, his family was taken from their home in Poland and sent to a concentration camp in Nazi Germany. Young Herman was forced to work shoveling bodies into a crematorium. All the while he did not know if he, too, would soon be killed.

After two years of unimaginable labor, Herman walked up to the barbed wire fence and saw a young girl on the other side.

"What are you doing in there?" the young girl asked.

Scared and starving, Herman whispered, "Can you give me something to eat?"

Facing possible death if caught, amazingly the girl took an apple and small piece of bread out of her jacket and handed it to Herman.

The girl fed Herman an apple every day for seven months. Then one day he told her not to come back—he was being moved to another camp. Both began to cry as they realized they would never see each other again.

Herman was shipped to Czechoslovakia. Just two hours before he was scheduled to die in the gas chambers, Russian troops liberated the camp and Herman was set free.

Many years later, in 1957, Herman was then living in New York City. A friend set him up on a blind date with a woman named Roma Radzika. Herman says that on the date he was immediately drawn to this young woman. When they began talking about their lives, Roma asked where Herman was during the war. He explained that he had been in a concentration camp. Roma then shared that her family had lived close by a camp and that she had snuck out every day to give a boy an apple and bread.

Her story hit Herman like a ton of bricks.

"There was a boy?" Herman asked bewildered. "Was he tall?"

Confused, Roma nodded.

"Did this boy tell you not to come around anymore?" Herman's voice trembled. "Because he was leaving—that he was being moved to another camp?"

"Yes." An incredulous smile crept across Roma's face.

"That boy was me," Herman explained, tears running down his cheeks.

"I know."

Roma and her family had moved from Poland to Germany, using forged papers to hide that they were Jewish. They lived on a farm next to Herman's camp, posing as Christians to avoid being captured. Roma explained that when she brought apples and bread for Herman, he used to say, "I'll see you tomorrow."

"Tomorrow" came fourteen years after their tearful good-bye at the fence.

"What can I tell you?" Herman told Oprah. "I proposed right there in that restaurant."

In the restaurant Herman took Roma's hand and looked into her eyes. "I'll never let you go anymore. Now that we are free I want us to be together forever."

Since that day their love has continued to grow. Herman and Roma have now been married for nearly fifty years.

Herman and Roma are a beautiful metaphor for what love can be. Oprah said they represent endurance, fate, and destiny. We have a slightly different perspective on it than she does. We say Herman and Roma represent God's desire for love and marriage. More than that, they represent God's amazing provision: "We know that God causes all things to work together for good to those who love God, to those who are called according to His purpose" (Romans 8:28 NASB). (This verse especially applies to Shawn and Christina who met in a bar.)

You and I may not have such a miraculous love story like Herman and Roma, but every couple has its own amazing stories, events, and memories of how two people came to be joined together as one by the Creator of this universe. We all have our own version.

How often do you and your spouse reminisce about your life together? Has it been awhile since you shared your love story? If so, one of the best things you can do for your marriage is to talk about your special memories. There is amazing power in recalling special locations, watching videos, looking at old pictures from your wedding and life together, or listening to your special songs.

Dr. John Gottman was able to predict with 94 percent accuracy which couples were going to divorce based solely on how they had answered questions about their marriage's history three years earlier. This strongly suggests a link between how a couple perceives its marital history and its likely future. Why? People who are feeling distressed more easily remember negative episodes from the past. So the couple's current negativity triggers negative memories that reinforce their current feelings.[14]

Reminiscing about the good times in a marriage can help strengthen the bond between husband and wife and draw them closer together. Recalling memorable events also provides hope through the anticipation for similar enjoyable times in the future. It helps you remember happier times and reminds you of the qualities that first attracted you to each other. It causes couples to say, "We're actually quite good together!"

Reminiscing about the special times in your marriage is easy. As you stroll down memory lane, we have one rule: your conversation must focus on the positive aspects of your experiences. Don't use this time to criticize, be negative, or use "slam" humor. Ask each other these questions to get you started:

- What first attracted you to me?
- What was going through your mind on our first date?
- When did you know I was the one you wanted to marry?
- What were some of your favorite parts of our marriage proposal?
- What was your reaction when you first found out we were pregnant?
- Beyond the obvious, what were some of the things you enjoyed on our honeymoon?
- What is your most favorite meal that I make? Why?
- What has been your most positive religious experience during the years of our marriage?
- What three things have you done during our marriage that you are most proud of?
- Over the last five years, how do you think you have changed for the better?
- What would you consider to be "our song"? Why is it so meaningful to you?
- In what ways do you feel blessed in our marriage?

♡ What is the best gift I've ever given you? Why was it so special?

♡ What are some of your favorite Valentine's Day memories?

♡ What do I do that is the biggest turn-on for you?

♡ What outfit of mine is your favorite? Why is it your favorite?

♡ What has been your most favorite church we've attended? Why?

♡ What is your most favorite piece of furniture or appliance we've bought together? Why?

♡ What is your favorite tradition that we've started? Why?

♡ What's been your most favorite house or place we've lived? Why?

♡ What are some of the best vacations we've taken together? Why?

♡ What are some of your favorite date-night activities we've done?

♡ What are some things that I've done for you that really made you feel loved?

♡ What would you consider as our "special place"? Why is it so meaningful to you?

♡ What's the most romantic thing I've ever done for you?

♡ What are some of your favorite Christmas memories?

♡ How do you tell our love story? What is your version?

Most couples find this kind of reminiscing enjoyable and enlightening. It reminds them that at one time they had some pretty wonderful feelings for each other. The power of reminiscing about your marriage and life together is that it inspires and motivates both of you, helps you recall the mutual love and trust you felt for each other, promotes hope and positive feelings about your relationship, rebonds you as a couple, takes you back to the important traits you enjoyed about each other, reminds you of the things that attracted you to each other, and provides a good laugh.

Tip #4: Protect Your Fun Activities from Conflict

In our marriage, Erin and I have had to protect our fun time. We consider this one of the most important boundaries we've established. And we learned how to protect fun experiences the hard way.

Early in our marriage Erin and I planned to spend a day at Disneyland. Before entering the park, we decided to save money by eating at a nearby sandwich shop. While I stuffed my mouth with a foot-long sub, I brought up a very sensitive issue, and an argument erupted. As the conflict escalated, we moved our "lively discussion" to the car, hoping to resolve the dispute without involving the entire restaurant. Unfortunately, the privacy didn't help.

Having no desire to spend the day walking around the "happiest place on earth" together while we both fumed, we drove home in silence. It took the entire day to resolve the argument. The worst part is that we ruined our Disneyland date. Our special day trip had the potential to add so many precious memories into the history of our marriage. Instead, we were left with a very bitter taste in our mouths (and it had nothing to do with the sandwiches!).

Erin and I did what no married couple should ever do: we allowed conflict to infiltrate our fun. Letting conflict invade your recreation is like throwing a red shirt into the washer with white clothes. Even though it's only one small shirt, it can destroy an entire load of laundry by turning it pink (I've also learned this the hard way!). Likewise, even though you may be discussing only one tiny issue, if it is allowed to enter into your relaxation, the entire experience can be damaged.

Conflict can be destructive to your fun times because it intensifies negative emotions, painful memories flood into your awareness, and people get hurt and become frustrated. As this happens, it becomes virtually impossible to relax and enjoy each other. If this pattern repeats too often, your mate may lose the desire to do fun things because the experience ends up turning "pink."

Before your enjoyment is destroyed, interrupt arguments or sensitive discussions by agreeing to talk about the issue at a later time. Reschedule the conversation when you can provide the necessary attention it deserves—and when it won't mess up the fun time you've got planned. Simply say, "Let's not do this right now. How about we talk about that issue later when we're back at home?"

The key is that you *must* deal with the conflict issue later, or your spouse won't trust that you'll ever talk about it again. Instead, he or she will express those negative feelings during your date because past experience has been that it will be his or her only opportunity.

By not allowing conflict to harm your recreation, you are sending a very important message: "Our relationship is more important than impulsively arguing about a problem."

Though we have encouraged you to laugh and have fun together, realize that humor does have some potential disadvantages. Probably the greatest one is the risk of using humor to deflect important issues—a serious conversation needs to take place, but one of you keeps putting it off with jokes.

Humor can also be used as a weapon to belittle others or score points in some fashion. You can use humor at the expense of someone, but let it be yourself rather than your spouse. When humor is used as a means of demeaning your spouse as a way to protect yourself from responsibility ("I was only joking"), your marriage is put at risk. Use humor with care. It is great for a relationship, but misuse of it can be toxic.

HAVE FUN!

Fun, laughter, and play with our spouses can be difficult because we all have more to do than can be done in each day. However, we need to develop the ability to separate ourselves from work, kids, and other responsibilities in order to have the possibility for enjoyment.

A wholehearted marriage is built when spouses keep their work and play in perspective—when they feel no remorse by relaxing, laughing, and having fun.

When was the last time you and your spouse enjoyed a healthy dose of fun and laughter? Erin and I made a commitment that our relationship would never lose that sense of fun. So we've made it a priority—we even schedule it on our calendars.

Spend time together talking about your dreams, telling stories, laughing, and just hanging out with each other. You need time to do all of those things you remembered doing when you fell in love. Laughing and having fun is also a way to appreciate those unique gifts each of you brings to the marriage, to forget petty resentments and, for a brief time, to let tomorrow take care of itself.

Conclusion
Walking It Out

Our deepest fear is not that we are inadequate. Our deepest fear is that we are powerful beyond measure. It is our light, not our darkness, that most frightens us. We ask ourselves, "Who am I to be brilliant, gorgeous, talented, or fabulous?" Actually, who are you not to be? You are a child of God. Your playing small does not serve the world. There is nothing enlightened about shrinking so that other people won't feel insecure around you. We were born to manifest the glory of God that is within us. . . . And as we let our own light shine, we unconsciously give other people permission to do the same. As we are liberated from our own fear, our presence automatically liberates others.

—Marianne Williamson

WHILE GREG teaches classes in the cold Ozark mountains of Northwest Arkansas, I (Shawn) am enjoying white-sand beaches, clear blue-green ocean water, tropical vegetation, and all-you-can-eat buffets at a wonderful resort in Cancun, Mexico.

It's not that I am celebrating the end of this book without him or that I am taking a fall vacation; the entire family is down here for my sister's wedding. She is a remarkable woman marrying a great guy.

She and I do not always see things the same way, but we can agree on one thing: marriage was designed to be engaged wholeheartedly. She is about to commit to a guy who is committing to her—not just a commitment to stay together, but a promise that they will fully engage themselves in this marriage.

These tropical destinations are a great place to watch families play. This resort has amazing swimming pools, a lazy river, waterfalls cascading into hot tubs, and a wave pool. The siren above the wave pool buzzes, signaling they are about to turn on the wave maker. People scamper to the pool. The two-foot waves begin. Some people float, some bob up and down, some dive under. Laughter and fun all around.

I have walked past these same families for three days in a row at the wave pool. They are content here. One thing intrigues me about the scene, though. Less than a hundred yards away there is a white-sand beach next to the most beautiful ocean I have ever seen. Visibility on most days in the clear blue water is as good as it is in the wave pool. But the waves are different. Five-footers crash in with beauty and force.

Some families elect to come here. They leave the safety of the hotel pool and come out to experience the thrill of the big waves. Here, like back at the resort, you can float, bob up and down, or dive under—but unlike at the hotel pool, you can *ride* these waves. Get on a surfboard or just stretch out on your belly, and you can really shoot on top of the water. It's a lot scarier here than at the wave pool, but so much more exhilarating.

You have the same choice. You can stay content at the imitation wave pool of an "adequate" marriage, or you can dive into the ocean of wholehearted marriage. You can live life safely, content with "getting by," or you can fully experience the marriage you have always wanted.

Wholehearted living does not mean you turn your brain off and just go play. On the contrary, your brain has to be fully engaged as well. Having a wholehearted marriage is a choice you make with your heart and your brain.

So what do you think? Are you ready to fully engage your heart in your marriage? Are you willing to get in the game—or are you going to stay on the sideline? Are you ready to take some risks, or do you want to keep playing it safe? You choose.

If you chose a wholehearted marriage, you are in for quite a ride. You will get to experience a depth of emotions you may have never felt before. Joy will be wonderful. Grief will be hard. But you will be fully alive. The Enemy will come against you by trying to tap into old wounds, pushing old buttons, creating new fears, and rushing you through life. But you have the ability to counter with the truth about who you are, an understanding of what healthy relationships look like, and a commitment to slow down and simplify.

The benefits to your marriage will be immeasurable. You and your spouse will feel more understood. Compassion and encouragement will flow naturally. Giftings and talents will be celebrated. In a wholehearted environment, your heart will be free to explore and be known. You will finally experience true intimacy and passionate connection with your spouse.

But you won't stop there. Living wholeheartedly will allow you to have genuine fellowship and community with the family and friends around you. You will be able to leave the baggage of your past and fully live the life God designed and intended for you.

Wholehearted living will allow you to serve the Lord completely. Think of the power of a large group of wholehearted people completely sold out to serving the Lord. There could be revival in our churches led by authentic people attracting and ministering to the lost.

Wow. Sorry. I got a little ahead of us. All of that may come. What matters first is you and your marriage.

Let's simplify it. Recognize the important role your heart plays in life. Pay attention to your heart: understand it, value it, take care of it, and use it. Fight against anything robbing you of living wholeheartedly, be it past wounds, fears, a hectic pace of life, or too much clutter. Let the care, compassion, encouragement, and fun that is in your heart to bless your spouse be unleashed.

Wholeheartedly engage your marriage. You are worth it. Your spouse is worth it. Your marriage deserves it. You will love it.

Notes

Introduction: The Heart of Marriage
1. Jim Collins, *Good to Great: Why Some Companies Make the Leap . . . and Others Don't* (New York: Harper Business, 2001).

Chapter 1—Heart 101
1. Biblegateway.com keyword search: love (NIV).

2. Dallas Willard, *Renovation of the Heart: Putting on the Character of Christ* (Colorado Springs: NavPress, 2002), 30.

3. www.the-tabernacle-place.com/tabernacle_articles/tabernacle_holy_of_holies.aspx. Accessed 11/6/08.

4. Philip S. Chua, *Know Your Heart*, Heart to Heart Talk, February 9, 2004, www.feu-nrmf.ph/drchua/pdf/K/KnowYourHeart.pdf.

5. Biblegateway.com keyword search: heart (NKJV).

6. John Eldredge, *Waking the Dead: The Glory of a Heart Fully Alive* (Nashville: Nelson, 2006), 34–39.

7. www.heartmath.org/index.php?option=com_content&task=view&id=28&Itemid=51. Accessed 11/6/08.

8. Eldredge, *Waking the Dead*.

Chapter 2—The Voice of the Heart
1. Gordon T. Smith, *The Voice of Jesus: Discernment, Prayer, and the Witness of the Spirit* (Downers Grove, IL: InterVarsity, 2003), 57.

2. Eldredge, *Waking the Dead*, 42–43.

3. Michael Gurian, *Boys and Girls Learn Differently* (San Francisco: Jossey-Bass, 2001); Arthur Horne and Mark Kiselica, eds. *The Handbook of*

Notes

Counseling Boys and Adolescent Males: A Practitioner's Guide (Thousand Oaks, CA: Sage, 1999), 8; Daniel Kindlon and Michael Thompson, *Raising Cain* (London: Penguin Books, 1999), 4, 12; William Pollack, *Real Boys: Rescuing Our Sons from the Myths of Boyhood* (New York: Henry Holt, 1998), 3; Terrence Real, *I Don't Want to Talk about It: Overcoming the Secret Legacy of Male Depression* (New York: Fireside, 1998); P. West, *Fathers, Sons, and Lovers* (Sydney: Finch, 1996), 212.

4. Dr. Ron Levant, a professor at Harvard University, teaches that most North American males suffer to some degree from the conditioning of our culture, which causes men to be underdeveloped emotionally.

5. 2001 Gallup poll; R. W. Osborne, "Men and Intimacy: An Empirical Review," in symposium conducted at the annual meeting of the American Psychological Association, San Francisco, 1991; as cited in Ronald Levant, "Toward the Reconstruction of Masculinity," *Journal of Family Psychology* 5, no. 3 & 4 (March–June 1992), 388.

6. Michelle Froese, "Women and Anger," www.essortment.com/all/womenanger_rkjc.htm.

7. Chip Dodd, *The Voice of the Heart: A Call to Full Living* (Franklin, TN: Sage Hill, 2001), 35.

8. www.answers.com/topic/emotion?cat=health, accessed 11/6/08 and en.wikipedia.org/wiki/Emotion. Accessed 11/6/08.

9. Carl Gustav Jung and Edward Hoffman, *The Wisdom of Carl Jung* (New York: Citadel, 2003), 87.

10. Dorothy C. Finkelhor, *How to Make Your Emotions Work for You* (Berkeley, CA: Medallion, 1973), 23–24.

11. www.theocentric.com/spirituality/prayer/songs_from_the_heart emotions.html. Accessed 11/6/08.

12. Archibald Hart, *Unlocking the Mystery of Your Emotions* (Dallas: Word, 1979), 15.

13. James Houston, *The Heart's Desire* (Vancouver, BC: Regent College Publishing, 2001), 112.

14. Gary Oliver, *Real Men Have Feelings Too* (Chicago: Moody, 1997), 45.

15. G. P. Hodgkinson, J. Langan-Fox, and E. Sadler-Smith, "Intuition: A Fundamental Bridging Construct in the Behavioural Sciences." *British Journal of Psychology* 99, no. 1 (2008): 1–27.

16. Richard Pellegrino, *The Complete Idiot's Guide to Improving Your IQ* (Royersford, PA: Alpha, 1998), 202.

17. Haim G. Ginott, *Between Parent and Child: New Solutions to Old Problems* (New York: Macmillan, 1965), 34–35.

Notes

Chapter 3—The Wounded Heart
1. Eldredge, *Waking the Dead.*

Chapter 4—The Fearful Heart
1. Archibald D. Hart and Sharon Hart Morris, *Safe Haven Marriage: Building a Relationship You Want to Come Home To* (Nashville: Nelson, 2003), 28.

2. Barbara De Angelis, *What Women Want Men to Know* (New York: Hyperion, 2001), 117.

3. De Neen L. Brown, "The Impassive Bystander," *Washington Post,* Wednesday, July 16, 2008, CO1.

Chapter 5—The Exhausted Heart
1. Nancy Gibbs, "How America Has Run Out of Time," *Time,* April 24, 1989, 59.

2. Richard Swenson, *Margin* (Colorado Springs: NavPress, 2004), 13, 61–63.

3. Al Menconi, "If Satan Wanted to Capture Our Attention, How Would He Do It?" www.almenconi.com/articles.php?art_id=159.

4. Les and Leslie Parrott, *Your Time-Starved Marriage: How to Stay Connected at the Speed of Life* (Grand Rapids: Zondervan, 2006), 39.

5. John Ortberg, *The Life You've Always Wanted* (Grand Rapids: Zondervan, 2002), 76.

6. Charles Swindoll, *Intimacy with the Almighty* (Nashville: Nelson, 2000), 4.

7. Jill Briscoe, www.parsonage.org/articles/married/A00000026.cfm. Accessed 11/6/08.

8. Swenson, *Margin,* 169.

9. Joyce Meyer, *100 Ways to Simplify Your Life* (New York: FaithWords, 2008).

10. Elaine St. James, *Simplify Your Life: 100 Ways to Slow Down and Enjoy the Things That Really Matter* (New York: Hyperion, 1994).

11. Rick Warren, *The Purpose-Driven Life* (Grand Rapids: Zondervan, 2002), 17.

12. Max Lucado, *It's Not About Me* (Nashville: Nelson, 2004).

13. Max Lucado, *Cure for the Common Life* (Nashville: Nelson, 2008).

14. Swenson, *Margin,* 77.

15. Doris Janzen Longacre, *Living More with Less* (Scottsdale, PA: Herald, 1980), 210–11.

Chapter 6—Caring for Your Mate's Heart

1. John Gottman, *Why Marriages Succeed or Fail* (New York: Simon & Schuster, 1994).

2. Howard Markman, Scott Stanley, and Susan Blumberg, *Fighting for Your Marriage* (San Francisco: Jossey-Bass, 2001), 92.

3. David Olson, Amy Olson-Sigg, and Peter Larson, *The Couple Checkup* (Nashville: Nelson, 2008), 34.

4. Steven Stosny, "Love without Compassion Is Possessive, Controlling, and Dangerous," www.compassionpower.com/anger%20lovewithoutcompassion.php.

5. Simon Baron-Cohen's *The Essential Difference: Men, Women and the Extreme Male Brain* (New York: Penguin Books, 2004).

6. www.glennrowe.net/BaronCohen/EmpathyQuotient/EmpathyQuotient.aspx. Accessed 11/7/08.

Chapter 7—Speaking to Your Mate's Heart

1. www.merriam-webster.com/thesaurus/encourage. Accessed 11/7/08.

2. Marcus Buckingham and Curt Coffman, *First, Break All the Rules* (New York: Simon & Schuster, 1999), 99.

3. Marcus Buckingham and Donald Clifton, *Now, Discover Your Strengths* (New York: Free Press, 2001).

4. David and Teresa Ferguson and Chris and Holly Thurman, *Intimate Encounters* (Nashville: Nelson, 1994), 12.

5. Gary Chapman, *The Five Love Languages* (Chicago: Northfield, 1995).

Chapter 8—Celebrating with Your Mate's Heart

1. Markman, Stanley, and Blumberg, *Fighting for Your Marriage*, p. 250.

2. Dolores Curran, *Traits of a Healthy Family* (New York: Ballantine, 1984), 143.

3. R. A. Martin and N. A. Kuiper, "Daily occurrence of laughter: Relationship with age, gender, and Type A personality." *Humor: International Journal of Humor Research* 12 (1999): 355–84.

4. L. Berk, "The Laughter-Immune Connection: New discoveries," *Humor and Health Journal* 5, no. 5 (1996): 1–5.

5. Berk, "Laughter-Immune."

6. Robert Provine, *Laughter: A Scientific Investigation* (New York: Penguin Books, 2001).

7. J. Killick, "Funny, Sad & Friendly: a drama project in Scotland," *Journal of Dementia Care*, Jan/Feb 2003, 24–26.

Notes

8. David C. Cook, *God's Little Devotional Book for Dads* (Tulsa, OK.: *Honor Books*, 1995), 10.

9. John M. Gottman, *The Seven Principles for Making Marriage Work* (New York: Crown, 1999), 79.

10. Ibid., 81.

11. Ibid., 80.

12. Ibid., 260.

13. "Reinventing Date Night for Long-Married Couples," www.nytimes.com/2008/02/12/health/12well.html. Accessed 11/7/08.

14. Gottman, *Why Marriages Succeed or Fail*, 128.

Conclusion: Walking It Out

Epigraph. Marianne Williamson, *A Return to Love: Reflections on the Principles of a Course in Miracles* (New York: Harper Collins, 1992), 190–91.

ABCs
THE
Authors, Book & Conversation

DR. GREG SMALLEY
DR. SHAWN STOEVER
THE AUTHORS

Dr. Greg & Erin Smalley

smalleymarriage.com

visit our website for

{

marriage tips

free resources

additional books

speaking request

marriage blog

smalleymarriage.com

What inspired you to write *The Wholehearted Marriage*?

This book was certainly inspired by our own life stories and circumstances. I (Greg) had reached a place a few years ago where there was a lot of personal and professional turmoil. I was struggling in a family-owned business, I felt burned out and massively depressed. I really didn't recognize that my heart had shut down. Even though I had been trained to help people manage depression, the skills and tools didn't work. For the first time in my life I couldn't "think" my way out of feeling depressed. God literally brought me to the point that I couldn't use my head to solve the crisis and He revealed to me that this was a heart issue. Fortunately, someone recommended the book *Waking the Dead* by John Eldredge. The book gave me words to describe what I was grappling with and feeling. This began my journey of questioning the role of my brain and my heart—especially my heart. I realized I had only been existing in my head, killing off my marriage, my relationships, and myself. As I learned to understand the importance of an open heart, how to care for it and keep it fully open, I came out of that deep, dark depression. Better yet, I no longer felt burned out and I recaptured God's call upon my life. My relationship with Christ, my wife, kids, family, and friends went to a new depth in terms of intimacy and connection. The best way to describe it is that my heart awakened!

We began to apply these concepts in our work with couples in crisis. We recognized that hearts were disconnected, shut-down, and generally ignored in epidemic proportions. By focusing our efforts in helping these crisis couples understand the necessity of reengaging their hearts, we began to see dramatic results. We watched in amazement as couples who had previously wanted to divorce began to get excited about the prospects of a truly connected and intimate marriage.

Since these concepts were changing our marriages and helping couples in crisis, we wanted to share these insights with others.

What do you see when you look at the landscape of marriage in America today?

In general, the message we hear regarding marriage in America is very negative—children are being raised without a mom and dad in the home, young couples are choosing cohabitation over marriage, and those who are married report high levels of dissatisfaction. None of this seems very honoring to an institution that means so much to the Lord.

Even with that said we are more optimistic and excited today than ever before. Marriage is a hot topic in so many different sectors of society. Politically, government is getting involved in healthy marriage initiatives and investing tax dollars in strengthening marriages. In the corporate world, business leaders are recognizing that unhealthy marriages and divorce cost them millions of dollars every year. Human resource departments are beginning to invest considerable time and energy into strengthening relationships within the workplace. In churches, leaders are recognizing that marriage is God's idea and something must be done to help members of their congregations cultivate Christlike marriages. All together, the issue of marriage in America seems to be reaching a tipping point. We appear to be on the verge of a marriage revival. The desire and movement towards healthy, thriving, wholehearted marriages can be contagious.

How can we maintain a wholehearted relationship even in changing economic times?

With the strain of financial pressure, job losses, and continual bad news on the television, stress on marital relationships may be at an all-time high. Now more than ever it is important to focus on having a solid relationship in the home. Spouses need to recognize they are on the same team, working together to overcome these hardships. While resources may be tight, strengthening your relationship doesn't have to cost any money. Building your relationship with your spouse and with the Lord will provide you with the solid foundation needed to face and overcome external circumstances that would otherwise leave us feeling helpless.

What separates couples with wholehearted marriages from the rest? How do they look different?

While we are not advocating that you diagnose your friend's marriages as wholehearted or halfhearted, it is usually fairly simple to see the results of a wholehearted marriage. In general, wholehearted couples rejoice and celebrate together—expressing joy, laughing, and experiencing adventure in their relationship. On the flip-side, wholehearted couples also mourn, hurt, cry, and empathize with each other. Simply put, hearts are fully engaged and connected in all seasons of life. Below is a chart to help further distinguish between the two ends of the spectrum:

Closed hearted:	Wholehearted:
Lifeless	Energized
Disconnected	Connected
Apathetic	Empathetic
Callous	Compassionate
Surviving	Thriving
Detached	Involved
Unavailable	Engaged
Selfish	Selfless
Uncaring	Loving
Distant	Close
Insensitive	Concerned
Reacting	Responding
Harsh	Gentle
Cruel	Kind

Given that this book is decidedly "Christian," how would someone who is not a Christian or from a different religious background live wholeheartedly?

Our bias is that everyone needs to have a personal relationship with Christ. That said, there is obviously evidence of many non-Christians who have a successful marriage with high levels of satisfaction. When hearts are open, love is free to flow. We believe God gave everyone a heart and the ability to open or close it, thus all of us are free to take advantage of this principle. Wholehearted, healthy people are able to give and care for others freely.

As a major distinction, people with a personal relationship with God understand the opportunity to get their needs met first and foremost from Him.

They are also free to receive and share His love. This combination creates the formula for the greatest marriages.

What personal challenges and obstacles do you face in keeping your hearts open?

We would both say that in the early stages of exploring these concepts, wounds and lies from our past were our biggest obstacles. As we have found healing in these areas, they no longer have the power to close our hearts down. Like many of the people we encounter on a daily basis, our biggest obstacle to maintaining wholehearted marriages today is the hectic, busy pace of our lives. Even as we teach and write, we recognize the enemy at work to prevent us from slowing down. At warp speed, we miss out on chances to wholeheartedly engage our wives, open our hearts for intimate sharing, and have fun without interruptions. However, we are committed to simplifying our lives so that wholehearted marriage becomes a way we live and not just a place we visit.

We recognize our wives are much further along in opening their hearts, and they have been our greatest teachers in this journey. Below we have included their answers to the following questions.

What do your wives think about you writing a book called *The Wholehearted Marriage*?

Our husbands' writing a book called *The Wholehearted Marriage* makes sense because that is how they live life. They have worked hard to get rid of obstacles that were blocking them from living "wholeheartedly." God has restored many areas of heartache, rejection, and loss that kept them from living up to their full potential. Both are men who really strive to make their relationship with the Lord, their marriages, and family a top priority.

What differences have you seen in your marriage as a result of your husband applying this material?

Christina Stoever: I won't lie and tell you that we apply these concepts all the time, but it definitely has made us aware of where we want to be. Our middle son Cade reminded us a couple of weeks ago, "Why don't you practice what you teach to the couples at the retreat." Great words! Our kids keep us humble. It really is a good thing to be reminded to stay the course. Shawn's applying these principles has made a difference in his personal life and in our marriage.

Erin Smalley: There was a great transition when Greg became more aware of his heart, and I am very proud of his spiritual growth. He seems to be more alive than I've seen him in years—talk about building safety in our marriage. It truly allowed a new level of intimacy to be uncovered in our relationship; instead of being a bystander, he became a wholehearted participant. Although he is not perfect, he blesses me and our family daily with his vibrant sense of humor and heartfelt caring.

Thank you for pursuing God wholeheartedly! We are blessed to be loved and cherished by our husbands.

For an exciting interactive online experience with the authors including video commentary, humorous and thought-provoking video illustrations visit WholeheartedMarriage.jlog.com powered by.

j›Log™
Let The Journey Begin

Discussion Group Guide

1.   What areas of your life (work, kids, marriage, hobbies, relationship with God) are you most wholehearted? Which areas do not come as naturally? What stops you from living wholeheartedly?

2.   Were you raised in a home where your parents or significant role models taught you how important your heart is in life and in relationships? Why do you think people don't talk about the importance of our heart?

3.   What messages are young boys taught about manhood and emotions? What messages are young girls taught about womanhood and emotions? How might these two different ways of handling emotions impact a marriage?

4.   Read through 1 John 4:7–21. Where does love come from? Do you agree that the love we feel towards our spouse is not generated by us but comes from God?

5.   Where is your heart in your marriage at this time? Is it shut down completely? Is it fully open?

6.   To better understand your ability to be aware of your emotions, answer the following questions:
- Do I pay a lot of attention to how I feel?
- Do I notice my emotions as I experience them?
- What emotions do I frequently experience?
- What emotions are easy for me to express?
- What emotions are difficult for me to express?
- What emotions did I see expressed in my family growing up?
- What emotions were never expressed in my family growing up?
- Can I accurately name my feelings?
- Do I pay attention to my thoughts, beliefs, and actions that could be causing how I feel?
- Do I understand how my feelings influence my thoughts and actions?
- Am I aware of how my emotions impact my spouse?

7.   How do you typically manage painful or troublesome emotions from your spouse? Do you...
- Remain emotionally unaware or disconnect from his or her heart?
- Judge, criticize, or disapprove of their emotions?
- Stuff, ignore, overlook, or disregard their feelings?
- Minimize, rationalize, or discount their emotions?
- Completely trust their feelings or believe they are true fact?
- Follow their emotions blindly, mindlessly act on them, or impulsively being led by them?
- Recklessly spew or spray your feelings in response to them?

8.   Think back over any significant moments that you can recall from your childhood (traumatic events, disappointments, times you were hurt). What were

you feeling? What did you say to yourself or what message did you receive from the incident—what were the lies written on your heart? In what ways have you replaced those lies, messages, and fears with God's truth? Where are you in the process of getting healing?

9. In order for intimacy and deep connection to occur, hearts *must* be open. And your heart will only open when you feel emotionally safe. Answer these questions:
- What specific things do you do on a regular basis to nurture and care for your heart?
- Do you mostly feel open and emotionally available in your marriage or do you feel guarded and distant?
- How safe do you feel with your spouse?
- Can you trust your spouse with the deepest parts of your heart?
- On a scale of 0 to 10 (with 10 being the safest), how safe is your marriage for you and your spouse?
- How do you react when you feel unsafe?
- What does your spouse do that helps you feel safe in your marriage?
- How have you made it unsafe for your spouse?
- How do you damage the safety of your marital environment?

10. What does a typical day in your life look like? How much spare time, leisure time, and down time do you have every day? To what extent do you feel worn out, tired, exhausted, and depleted? What is the high cost you and your marriage are paying for a fast paced lifestyle? In what ways can you slow down and simplify your life?

11. How effective are you at opening your heart to be impacted by what your spouse is feeling? What keeps you from empathizing with your spouse? What might help you do a better job of really feeling your spouse's pain and other emotions?

12. God built things into the heart of your spouse that were designed to change the world. Which gifts, talents, and hidden abilities are stored in your spouse's heart that needs to be exposed? What is keeping you from calling out your spouse's amazing gifting?

13. What role does humor, laughter, and having fun play in your marriage? As the years go by, many couples slip into a rut of predictability. What are some ways that you could surprise your spouse by doing something unexpected?

14. Every couple has their own amazing stories, events, and memories of two people joined together as one by the creator of this universe. How often do you reminisce about your life together? Has it been a while since you shared your love story? What is keeping you from reminiscing about memorable things that have happened over the course of your marriage? What will you do to change this?